The practical guide to KNOTS

Selecting and tying the right knot for every situation

The practical guide to KNOTS

Selecting and tying the right knot for every situation

COLIN JARMAN

APPLE

Published by Apple Press
6 Blundell Street
London N7 9BH

ISBN 1 84092 329 6

TPKN

This book was designed and produced by
Quintet Publishing Limited
6 Blundell Street
London N7 9BH

Senior Project Editor: Laura Price
Designer: James Lawrence
Photographer: Jeremy Thomas
Art Editor: Sharanjit Dhol

Creative Director: Richard Dewing
Editorial Director: Jeremy Harwood

Manufactured in Hong Kong by Regent Pte Ltd.
Printed in China

Contents

Ropes and knots

1 Quick tie knots

2 Easy-release knots

Man has used some form of twisted fiber rope since he began tying sharp stones to pieces of stick for cutting tools or weapons and, as soon as he tried to attach the stone to the wood, he had to invent knots. However, the greatest development of

knots, and the time when the widest variety was produced, was in the days of sail when the great voyages of exploration took place, sailing navies ruled the world, and the great trade routes were established. Seamen relied on rope and knots to such an extent that they developed several thousand knots to meet their many different needs.

Since those productive days we have seen the waning of sailing ships and the development of synthetic fiber ropes, which together have changed the face of knotting and ropework. We now have to ensure security of our knots in materials that are immensely strong, yet extremely slippery, and we only use knots in a limited number of situations. We still need them, however, and this book sets out to provide a reference for the tying of the most practical and common knots, bends, and hitches, whether you need them for a simple, everyday job or a specialized one in fishing, camping, sailing, or climbing.

Top: Rope held taut in position through a block with a stopper knot.

Left: The Hunter's Bend is a useful knot which has a good grip and, although stable, is easy to untie.

Ropes and Knots

Choosing Ropes and Lines

Your choice of a rope or line will depend on several factors linked to the intended use and how much you are prepared to spend. There is, for example, no point in giving a rock climber a beautiful, hugely expensive rope made out of PBO if it breaks his back when he falls off the rock face because it does not stretch. However, a nylon rope might be just the thing, as its stretchiness will absorb the shock loads of his fall. In contrast, a new set of headsail sheets might make a great present for a boat owner, but not if they are made of stretchy nylon, as he will spend all his time tightening them in order to keep the sail trimmed properly. For this use a Polyester line will be far more appropriate.

Purpose	Material		
	Poly-propylene	Nylon	Polyester
General purpose			X
Climbing		X	
Towing	X	X	
Anchorage		X	X
Mooring	X	X	X
Halyards			X
Fishing		X	

CARE AND MAINTENANCE

Before deciding on which type of rope to buy, list the factors involved:
- Is stretch beneficial?
- Do you want a floating line?
- Is chafe resistance important?
- Will the line be exposed to large amounts of UV?
- Can the line be cheap and, therefore, "disposable"?
- Is there a line that is made for this particular purpose?
- Would color coding be a help?

Ropeworking terms

Jargon has been kept to a minimum in this book, but there are a few ropeworking terms for which it is hard to find substitutes. The main part of the rope that is generally inactive during knotting is called the standing part, while the part actually doing the moving around to form the knot is called the working end. A loop is a large, loose C formed in the rope; a bight is a flat, narrow loop. A crossed loop is a closed circle with one part crossing over the other

Opposite, clockwise from top: A Rolling Hitch attaches one line securely to another; A Grinner Knot is one of the best methods of tying a fly to a line; A Highwayman's Hitch is, as its name suggests, perfect for tethering a horse to a rail; A Figure Eight Loop is particularly suited to modern climbing harnesses and carabiners.

Rope Construction

The majority of rope today, whether intended for climbing or boating, is braided with a fairly smooth, woven appearance, unlike the twisted (laid) character of earlier and natural fiber ropes. Laid ropes are still available and have many uses, but they are no longer the most popular.

It is important to note that some synthetic materials are degraded by ultra violet light and require inhibitors to be included in their manufacture if they are to have a reasonable life expectancy. Indeed, some of the really advanced materials, such as Kevlar, Vectran, and PVO, are so sensitive to ultra violet light that they have to be stored in conditions of complete darkness until they are incorporated into the core of a rope and covered by its protective sheath.

BREAKING STRAINS

Various tables of breaking strains are available to help with choosing the right diameter of line for a particular job, but manufacturers are constantly changing their figures and it is wise to seek the most up to date information from them. However, for many applications strength is hardly a consideration; rather it is selecting a line of a thickness that will be comfortable to handle that is important. For example, the sheets on a family sailing cruiser need to be around ½ inch (12mm) in diameter to make them easy to control, but rope of that size will have a strength far beyond the loads such sheets will have to cope with. Where strength is critical, such as for fishing line, the lines are sold according to their breaking load, for example, as 20lb or 50lb line.

Diameter of Rope	Breaking Strains of Rope Types				
	3 strand Nylon	8 strand Nylon	8 plait Polypropylene	3 strand Polyester	Polyester with a braided core
4 mm	–	–	275 kg	500 kg	–
6 mm	750 kg	–	560 kg	940 kg	1230 kg
8 mm	1350 kg	1400 kg	1060 kg	1610 kg	1900 kg
10 mm	2800 kg	2400 kg	1400 kg	2100 kg	2300 kg
12 mm	3000 kg	3000 kg	–	3250 kg	3350 kg
14 mm	4100 kg	3800 kg	–	4200 kg	5100 kg

Nylon

The first synthetic material used for making ropes and lines, nylon is stretchy and strong, being particularly well-liked by climbers as it absorbs shock loads well, for example if someone falls from a rock face. Surprisingly, however, the strength of nylon is greatly reduced when it is wet. This reduction can be as much as 20 percent. Despite that, nylon remains a popular material and is still one of the stronger ones. Nylon is also used in monofilament form for fishing lines, where its strength allows the lines to be very fine.

Above: Nylon 3-strand

Above: Anchor braid

Above: Nylon braided core and sheath

Polypropylene

This extraordinarily versatile material is used mainly in three-strand laid form where it is found in five main varieties, all of which are relatively inexpensive. All polypropylene ropes float, are useful in a broad range of situations, but are vulnerable to chafe and ultra violet degradation:

Monofilament Polypropylene is the form most resistant to abrasion and general wear. It has a slippery, dull finish, which is not very easy to grip and the line feels hard.

Split-film Polypropylene has every appearance of being cheap and cheerful. If the ends of such lines are not whipped or sealed immediately after cutting they will unlay and spring open.

Staple-spun Polypropylene is rough and hairy, giving a good, but uncomfortable grip.

Multifilament Polypropylene produces a softer, more easily handled line that tends to hold knots better than some of the springier versions.

Fibrillated Polypropylene is produced in brown and looks like natural hemp fiber rope. Although cheap and cheerful, it is hard on the hands and is now largely replaced by buff spun polyester, which is softer and performs better on traditional sailing craft.

Above: 3-strand polypropylene monofilament

Above: Staple spun 3-strand

Above: Dyneema

Above: 3-strand staple spun

Above: Braid on braid

Polyester

Ropes and lines made from Polyester, which used to be sold under trade names such as Terylene and Dacron, are available in both braided and three-strand laid forms. They have almost the same ultimate strength as nylon lines, but stretch less, particularly in their pre-stretched form. Polyester lines do not float and are hardwearing.

Exotics

Beyond these common rope-making materials there are a number of very exotic fibres now in use, such as Dyneema, Spectra, Vectran and PBO. This last has more than five times the strength of Polyester, hardly stretches at all, but costs around 35 times as much! It's a very specialized material.

Above left: 16-plait matt polyester
Above: 3-strand pre-stretched polyester

Left: 3-strand polyester matt finish

Coiling or Storing

When they are not actually in use, ropes and lines need to be coiled and stored carefully to ensure quick access to them without time being wasted unknotting and sorting them out. A rope left lying around will tangle, trip people up and may be damaged, so coil and stow every time and to avoid snarl-ups when the coil is undone, always coil three-strand rope in neat clockwise loops and braided rope of any sort in figures of eight.

Above: Coiled ropes stored for easy access aboard a ship.

Three-strand, half hitch Coil: The simplest way of dealing with three-strand rope is to coil it and use the tail end to form a half hitch round the coils. In stiff or springy rope the half hitch will not be too secure unless the coiled rope is hung up by the tail used for the half hitch.

(a) Form the line into neat coils, laid up in a clockwise direction.

(b) With the last length of line form a much smaller loop at the top of the coils.

(c) Pass the end over the top of the coils and bring it forwards under them to come out through the small loop. Now the coil can be hung up by the remaining tail.

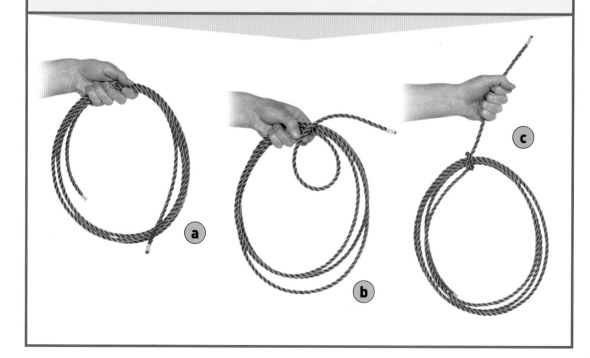

Buntline or Gasket Coil

1 First coil the rope in tidy figures of eight to avoid introducing twist, which will make the line snarl up when it is uncoiled.

2 At the end of the coil, use a length of the line to lay on a series of turns about the body of the coil, spiralling up towards the top.

3 With the binding turns in place, pass a loop of the line through the top of the coil.

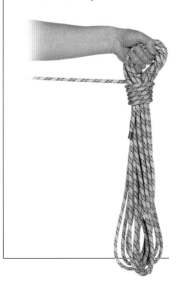

4 Spread the bight out and drop it down over the top of the coil and settle it on top of the binding turns.

5 Pull the end of the line tight, settling everything neatly together. The remaining tail of rope can be used to hang the coil up if required.

Self-Stopped Coil

These are two more ways of securing a coiled rope for storage. Both keep the rope tidy and secure, the first providing a tail to hang the coil by and the second providing a loop for the same purpose.

(1) Coil the rope in a series of figures of eight.

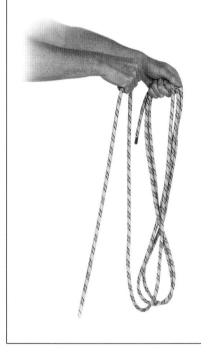

COILS IN ACTION

Settle everything down tightly and the coil is ready for storage.

(3) Use the tail of the line to bind the loop against the top of the coils, working towards the loop itself.

2 When the coil is completed, form a loop in the remaining line.

Variation:
(a) To finish the coil with a loop for hanging it up by, rather than a plain tail, coil the rope, form a loop at the top and then bind it to the coil using the tail doubled over into another loop.
(b) When the binding is complete, pass the second loop through the original loop.
(c) The coil is ready to be hung up.

4 Finish by passing the tail of the line through the loop.

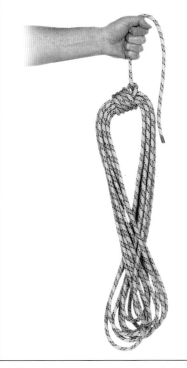

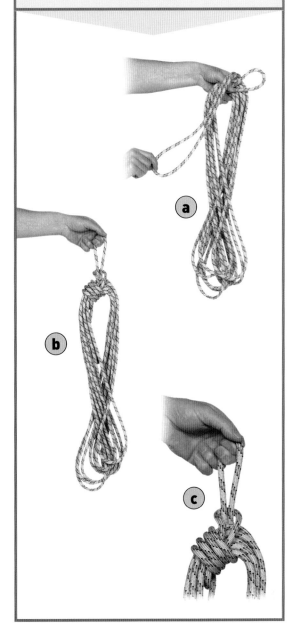

How to Use this Book

The knots in this book have been organized by physical properties rather than technical name. This means that you can find a range of knots ideally suited to the job in hand, whether this means a knot that can be easily tied, a quick-release knot, a sliding knot, or a knot that will remain firm under load. The introduction to each knot explains the background to the knot and, where applicable, its most common use. The icons shown for each knot serve as a quick reference for the knot's most practical uses, and the step-by-step photographs show the view that you will have as you tie the knot.

Using the icons

Climbing: Climbing knots tend to be very strong, hold well under load, and are usually easy to tighten and loosen.

Camping: Knots that hold firmly but do not require extensive rope working skills are particularly useful to campers.

Sailing: This is probably the widest category for knots. Each job on board may require a apecific style of knot.

General purpose: From packages to gardening, most knots can be applied to everyday use.

Fishing: The most specific category, for ease of use the step-by-step photographs have been shot using a fine rope rather than fishing line.

Quick tie knots

Overhand Knot

An Overhand Knot is one of the simplest and most basic knots. It can be used to stop a line running out through an eye or other fastening and it is the first step when forming several other knots, including the Reef knot, Surgeon's Knot, and the everyday "bow" used to tie shoelaces. It is often used in the end of sewing cotton to stop it pulling out through the material being stitched.

KNOTS IN ACTION

The finished overhand knot forms a useful, but quite small, stopper knot. If pulled really tight it may prove very hard to undo.

1 Pass the working end (with the colored tape) behind the main part of the line to form a crossed loop.

2 Bring the working end forward and down into the open loop.

3 Push the working end through the loop and pull the knot tight, adjusting the free end to a sensible length.

Double Overhand Knot

The Double Overhand Knot is a grown up version of the simple Overhand Knot (see opposite), which produces a more substantial "lump" in the rope or line to stop it running through an eye or block. When used in sewing cotton it will stop the thread pulling through material of a looser weave than will the single version.

1 Start by forming a single overhand knot then put an extra turn in by bringing the working end forward and down through the loop again.

2 Pull the working end through the loop so that it looks like this and draw the knot tight.

CARE AND MAINTENANCE

All rope needs to be looked after, either by way of protecting it from such things as chafe and abrasion or by coiling it up so that it is ready for use. If basic precautions are not taken, the rope may let you down disastrously at a crucial moment. It also makes economic sense to look after rope, as it will then last longer.

KNOTS IN ACTION

The extra turn makes a double overhand knot a bulkier one than the single version, so it is less likely to be pulled through an eye, block, or other restriction.

Clove Hitch

The Clove Hitch is designed to have nearly equal loads applied to both sides at the same time. It is not intended to be used where there is load on only one end, particularly if that load is going to move about. Should that happen, particularly with a line made of a slippery material, the Clove Hitch will eventually roll itself undone. It's an ideal hitch to use when setting up a temporary rope and post fence or running a grabline between several fixed points.

KNOTS IN ACTION

The finished clove hitch formed around a pole. Remember to apply loads equally (or nearly equally) to both ends at the same time.

1 Pass the working end of the line across the front of the pole, round behind it and then forward across the top.

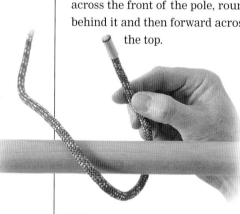

2 Bring the working end forward and across the standing part before sending it back behind the pole.

3 The working end is now brought forward over the top of the pole and tucked under the crossover beside the standing part.

4 The parts of the hitch are now brought together, settled and worked up tight, ready to take equal loads on each end.

Cow Hitch

The Cow Hitch provides a very simple way of hitching a line to a ring or pole with both ends left available for loading. These loads should be similar to prevent the rope slipping through the knot—one of the biggest problems with very slippery modern synthetics. The Cow Hitch is often used to secure sail ties to guardwires or grabrails.

KNOTS IN ACTION

A finished Cow Hitch with both ends ready for loading. After use, the hitch can be undone by pushing the rope loop away from the ring to loosen it.

1 Pass a bight of rope up through the ring

2 If the ring is free, like this one, the loop can be opened out and the ring passed through it. Otherwise, as shown, bend the loop back...

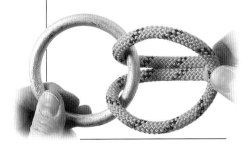

3 ...then pull the two ends of the rope up through it.

4 Settle hitch up against the ring and the two ends are ready for use.

Rolling Hitch

The Rolling Hitch is a development of the Clove Hitch (p24) and is an easy way of securing a line to either another rope or a pole when load will be applied in only one direction. While the Clove Hitch needs loads on both ends, the Rolling Hitch actually tightens with load applied to just one end.

When forming either style of Rolling Hitch, it is important to determine in which direction the load will eventually be applied as this dictates the direction in which the various turns must be made. The strain must be back against these turns, as can be seen in the pictures of the finished hitches.

1 Pass the working end of the rope back over the pole and start to bring it forward.

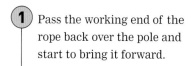

2 Wrap the working end of the rope right round the pole.

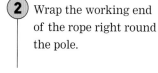

3 Make a second full turn round the pole with the working end.

4 Bring the working end forward; lead it across the front of the other turns then back behind the pole.

5 Finish by tucking the end under the crossover.

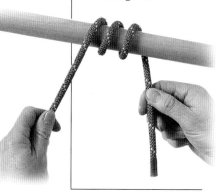

KNOTS IN ACTION

VARIATION: The two forms of this hitch differ only a little, but they do so significantly. The important fact is that the pole will not deform under load, while the rope will, as can be seen in the picture of the finished hitch. This change of shape (or lack of change) results in loads being transferred differently, hence the need for friction and binding to be achieved differently. Neither form is hard to learn, so it's worth taking the trouble to learn both.

With the turns of the hitch worked up tight so that they lie neatly side by side, it is easy to see the similarity to a Clove Hitch, the big difference being the Rolling Hitch's ability to accept a load on just one end of the rope.

a) Pass the working end of the rope back over the fixed line and bring it forward.

b) Lay a crossing turn over the standing part and bring the working end forward again.

c) Put another crossing turn over the standing part, again bringing the working end forward.

d) Lay on a last crossing turn and bring the end forward on the other side of the standing part.

e) Tuck the working end up beneath the final crossing turn to complete the hitch.

f) Settle all the turns neatly and tightly together, binding the standing part to the fixed line and apply load against these turns.

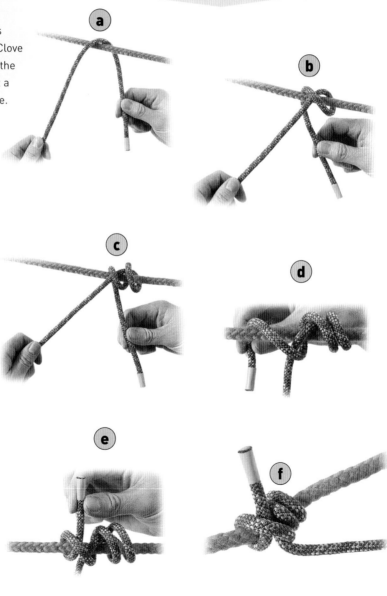

Figure-Eight Knot

This is an excellent stopper knot because it forms a good, big "lump" in the rope to stop it running through blocks or eyes, but generally remains quite easy to undo. If it has been under very heavy load, undoing may be a struggle, but it's still easier than an overhand knot. The key to its formation is the over-and-under weaving to form the figure eight; it doesn't matter in which direction it is done.

KNOTS IN ACTION

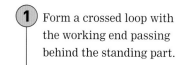

The finished Figure-Eight with a tail left long enough for it not to come undone, but not so long as to be a nuisance when the knot is against a block or eye.

1 Form a crossed loop with the working end passing behind the standing part.

2 Bring the working end forward and cross it back over the standing part.

3 Pass the working end up through the middle of the loop.

4 The over-and-under weaving results in this figure-eight shape just waiting to be worked up tight.

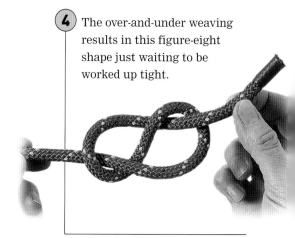

Half-tucked Blood Knot

Many anglers favor this knot for joining fine monofila-ment line to hooks and swivels, as it is easy to learn and quick to tie, besides being secure once settled. It is not particularly suited to larger lines, but for clarity in the illustrations we have used a light cord in which to tie the knot.

KNOTS IN ACTION

Work the entire knot up tight against the eye of the hook and cut the end of the line off leaving only a short tail.

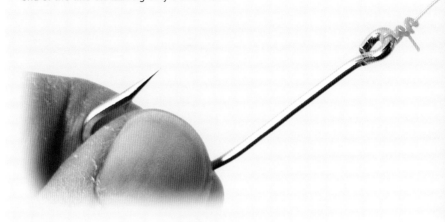

1 Pass the working end of the line through the eye of the hook then down and under the standing part.

2 Twist the working end round the standing part three times.

3 Take the working end back and thread it forward through the loop next to the eye.

4 Finish by tucking the working end back through between itself and the twists.

Heaving Line Bend

When a heaving line is used to send a larger warp across either from ship to shore or from one side of a river to the other, for example, it has to be secured to the warp. This bend is simple, quick to tie and, just as importantly, quick to release. It does not look as though it was devised by a great ropeworker, but it does its job.

1 If there is no loop spliced into the end of the heavier line, form a bight and lay the heaving line across the top. With the working end, go round the upper side of the loop, down and up between the loop and the heaving line's standing part.

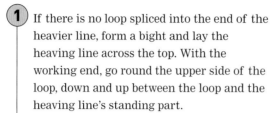

2 Cross the working end down under the lower part of the loop and up through the middle.

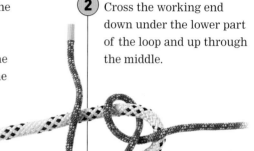

3 Send the end over the top part and back up into the middle.

4 Continue this weaving to and fro across the loop in the heavier warp.

KNOTS IN ACTION

Complete the bend by settling all the crossings up together so that they hold securely.

5 To finish, just bring the working end up through the center between the last two crossings.

Easy-release knots

Reef Knot (Square Knot)

This is one of the best-known knots, taking its common name from its nautical use for tying reef points when reefing (reducing sail area). The alternative name of Square Knot comes about because of its regular shape, even though it is more rectangular than square. Despite the Reef Knot's popularity it is often misused or tied incorrectly. It should never be used for joining two lines and care must be taken not to end up with a Granny Knot, which will either slip or jam completely.

KNOTS IN ACTION

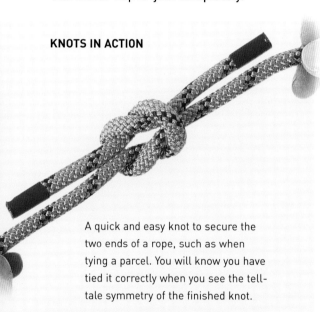

A quick and easy knot to secure the two ends of a rope, such as when tying a parcel. You will know you have tied it correctly when you see the tell-tale symmetry of the finished knot.

1 Start by crossing the end in your left hand over the one in your right.

4 Now cross the new right hand end over the new left hand end.

UNTYING: The beauty of this knot is that it will hold firm, but can be untied easily. As with any knot, you can untie it by simply reversing the tying action, but you can also push the loops together (a) to loosen the knot, or pull one end over the knot (b), keep going until that part of the rope is straight (c), then slip the remaining loops off (d).

(a)

2 Tuck the left (working) end down behind the right hand end

3 Bring the working end up to the front.

5 Tuck the right end down behind the left end and bring it forward through the center of the knot.

6 Pull the two ends to tighten the knot.

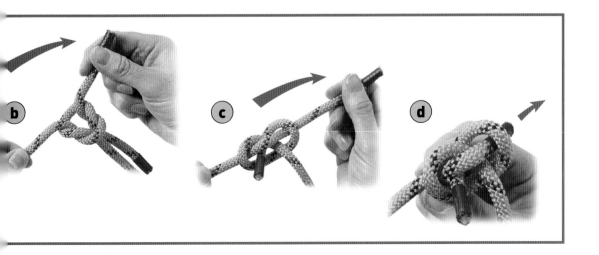

b   c   d

Slipped Reef Knot

The Slipped Reef Knot, or Half Bows is used to tie the two ends of a single piece of line together, not to join two lines. It makes sure an ordinary Reef Knot will be easy to undo when required. For example, a seaman may use it on sail tiers when stowing a sail to be sure that a quick tug on the slipped end will release the tier when the sail is needed in a hurry.

KNOTS IN ACTION

The finished knot with all parts settled down and pulled tight, leaving the slipped end available for quick release.

1 Start by forming a loose Reef Knot

2 Tuck one working end back through the knot, parallel to itself.

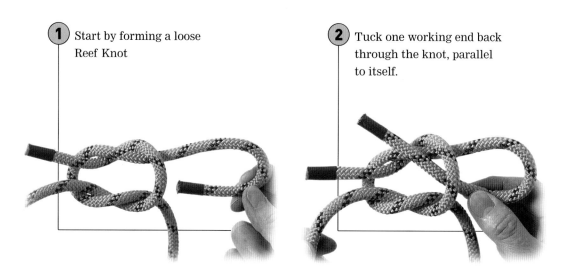

UNTYING: The knot is untied very easily by pulling on the slipped end. Once the loop is pulled clear the knot falls apart.

Double Slipped Reef Knot

Most people think of this knot as just "a bow" and use it to tie shoelaces. It's a perfectly good use for the knot and makes it, arguably, the most widely used knot we know. However, it has wider applications, being appropriate in many situations where the two ends of a single line need to be joined securely, but remain easily released.

KNOTS IN ACTION

Both ends of a Reef Knot have been tucked back through the body of the knot and the whole worked tight to form a "bow". As with the Reef Knot, it should not be used to join two separate lines, only to tie together the ends of the same line.

UNTYING: When the knot has to be undone, it is only necessary to pull on the two slipped ends to release it. Once the loops are pulled out the knot falls apart.
a. Grasp each loose end.
b. Pull ends away from one another.

Catspaw Hitch

This charmingly named hitch is ideal for securing a line or sling to a hook or pole (if the pole ends are available). It is best used with equal loads on each end and for added security when using particularly slippery line, an extra twist can be inserted.

CARE AND MAINTENANCE

Cleaning out sand, grit, and oily deposits from ropes helps to stop internal chafe and degradation. Use warm soapy water and a scrubbing brush or even put the ropes through a low temperature washing machine cycle. Once cleaned, allow the ropes to air-dry before coiling and storing them.

KNOTS IN ACTION

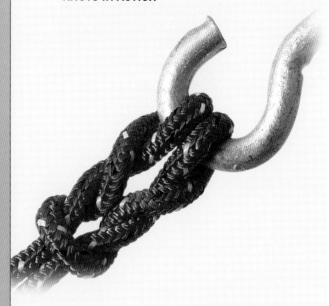

The finished Catspaw is slipped onto the hook and worked up tight, retaining the shape and form against the hook.

1 Form a bight in the line or flatten the sling into a loop.

4 Hold the ears by their tips and twist them outwards, so that the standing parts move to the outside.

2 Bend the top of the bight down, forwards, over the standing parts.

3 Now flatten out the two loops formed by step 2, so that they look like rabbit's ears.

5 Repeat the outward twisting on each side.

6 Turn the two small ears back to back and slip them onto the hook or, as shown here, your thumb so that you can begin to work the hitch tighter before transferring it to the hook.

QUICK RELEASE: The hitch will hold perfectly securely on the hook, particularly if equal loads are applied to each end, but when it's finished with, it can be slipped off the hook and it will immediately fall apart.

Highwayman's Hitch

The name of this hitch gives away its origins in horseback riding, though whether highwaymen actually used it or not is hard to tell. It is a secure way of hitching reins to a rail, but offers a quick getaway by pulling on the tail end to undo it. The hitch may, of course, be used in many other applications where a line needs to be released easily, using only one hand.

1 Pass a bight of the line up behind the rail.

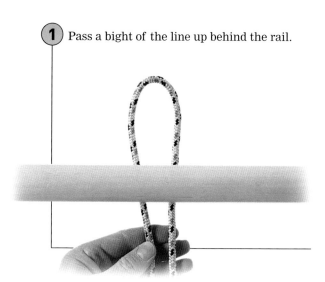

KNOTS IN ACTION

With everything settled down firmly, any tugging on the standing part (say as a horse moves about) serves only to tighten the hitch, but it only needs a good pull on the short end to free the hitch.

2 Loop the working end over in front of the bight.

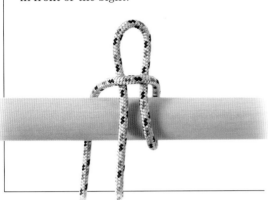

3 Bring the working end forwards beneath the rail.

4 Pull down on the working end to tighten the loop around the original bight and then form a new bight in the working end.

5 Pass this new bight up through the original one.

6 Pull down on the standing part of the line to tighten the original bight around the neck of the second bight.

Thief Knot

The Thief Knot is included here more for interest than practical use. That at least is the hope, for the knot was devised by sailors to catch a thief among their shipmates. At a quick glance the knot is a Reef Knot and a thief, pressed for time and likely to be spotted in the confines of the fo'c's'le, would replace it as such and so prove his existence. In happier circumstances it's quite a nice knot to puzzle youngsters with.

KNOTS IN ACTION

Having the same square shape and regularly woven pattern, it's very easy to mistake the Thief Knot for a Reef Knot—as was the intention. However, closer inspection shows that the ends emerge from the knot at diagonally opposite corners; in a Reef Knot they come out at corners on the same side.

1 Form a loop in one end of the line with the short end on top and pass the other (working) end up through it.

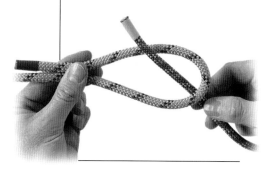

2 Lead the working end round the back of the loop and forward below it.

3 Weave the working end back through the loop to emerge parallel with its own standing part.

Hold-fast knots

Surgeon's Knot

Now called the Surgeon's Knot, this knot started out as the ligature knot with just a single twist in the second part, tied with forceps.

The addition of a second turn gives the knot a more regular form, rather like a Reef Knot with an extra twist on each side, and seems to make it hold better in thicker lines. However, in fine lines or monofilament fishing lines, it may be more effective to use the ligature style with a single turn in the second part. Either way, it holds slippery materials better than a Reef Knot.

KNOTS IN ACTION

The finished knot worked up tight with the twists in each side clearly defined. As with the Reef Knot, it is used to join the two ends of a single line, not to join two separate lines.

1 Twist the two working ends together in an overhand knot, using the "left over right" technique of the Reef Knot.

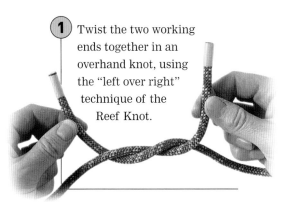

2 Use one of the ends to put in an extra turn.

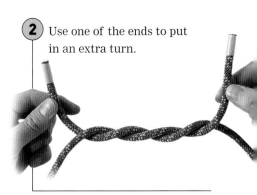

3 Now work back with a "right over left" movement to form the next overhand knot.

4 Use one end to put in an extra twist to match the first part of the knot before working the knot tight.

Round Turn & Two Half Hitches

It's a very long name for a simple and useful hitch. The name does, however, describe the hitch's formation exactly. All you do is apply a round turn followed by two half hitches. Easy! The Round Turn and Two Half Hitches is used for hitching a line to any ring, spar, pole, or post. It may not have quite the ultimate tenacity of the Anchor Bend, but it generally holds well and should be used for such purposes as hanging fenders from guardrails on boats in preference to the often seen Clove Hitch, which is definitely not meant for such use.

KNOTS IN ACTION

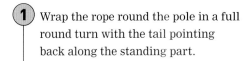

The finished Round Turn and Two Half Hitches provides a secure, simple way to hitch a line to a post, pole, or ring. If you examine the completed hitch you will see that the two half hitches are arranged to form a Clove Hitch about the standing part. Don't leave the tail too short if the rope is slippery.

1 Wrap the rope round the pole in a full round turn with the tail pointing back along the standing part.

2 Pass the working end over the standing part and tuck it through to form a half hitch.

3 Again pass the working end over the standing part, making sure that you do this in the same direction as the first time.

4 Tuck the working end through to form a second half hitch and settle everything tightly.

Timber Hitch

This is a handy and easily formed hitch for when you need to haul a log, branch or bit of lumber for any distance. It requires absolutely no knotting skill, but does its job perfectly. It will work in any size or type of line from the thinnest cord to the thickest cable; it even works in chain and wire.

(1) Take a turn round the timber with the working end of the line.

KNOTS IN ACTION

If you're going to haul the log or plank behind you, secure the Timber Hitch and then, as far away from it as possible, put a half hitch round the wood and lead your pull from that. This secondary hitch helps to keep the Timber Hitch itself in place and secure by maintaining the tension on it.

(4) Twist the working end round its own standing part several times.

2 Pass the working end behind the standing part and cross it over.

3 Tuck the working end under its own standing part, keeping tension on the main part of the line.

5 Tuck the working end between its own standing part and the timber so that it is locked in place by the pull on the main part of the line.

6 The Timber Hitch works by the friction in the twists, coupled with the locking pressure on the working end, so keep tension on the main part of the line at all times.

Halyard Hitch

Excellent for hitching a line to a pole or spar, this hitch derives its name from the days when halyards were bent onto the yard or gaff rather than being attached by a shackle. It's a neat, tidy looking hitch that binds tightly under load.

1 Begin by taking two full turns around the pole so that the working end points back parallel to the standing part.

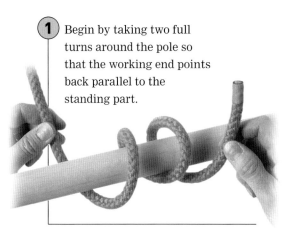

2 Lead the working end back behind the standing part.

KNOTS IN ACTION

Once the Halyard Hitch is settled, further loading while in use binds the turns and locks them more tightly, ensuring complete security. To undo the hitch, "break" the loop around the standing part and push some of the standing part through to slacken the turns on the pole.

3 Bring the end forward and tuck it under the turns laid on the pole, then pull the working end through, lengthening it if need be.

4 Finally, lead the working end back over the first turn and pass it under the next two.

Buntline Hitch

Usually used to attach a line to a ring, the Buntline Hitch could just as well be used on a pole or post. In either case it will slide until it is tight against the ring or pole and then lock against itself. The name derives from the lines that were attached to eyes (cringles) in the lower edge (foot rope) of a square sail and were used to gather the bunt (belly) of the sail up to the yard (the spar or pole it was hung from).

KNOTS IN ACTION

Settle the turns of the hitch together and pull it up tight against the ring where it will stay secure. When finished with, easing the load on the standing part will allow the hitch to be pulled away from the ring, loosened and undone.

1 Lead the working end of the line up through the ring and cross it over behind the standing part.

2 Bring the working end across in front of both parts.

3 Next pass the end back behind both parts.

4 To finish, tuck the working end down between the standing part and the crossover, then down through the loop.

47

Prusik Knot

The Prusik Knot takes its name from Dr Carl Prusik, who devised the knot for climbers in 1931. It is used to attach a sling, made of either rope or tape, to a standing line. The knot has the quality of locking on the standing line when load is applied to the sling, but of freeing enough to be moved when load is taken off it. Slings attached by Prusik Knot to a standing line can be used for climbing up the line.

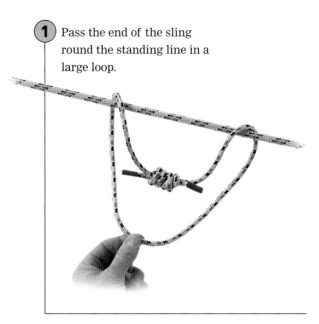

1 Pass the end of the sling round the standing line in a large loop.

KNOTS IN ACTION

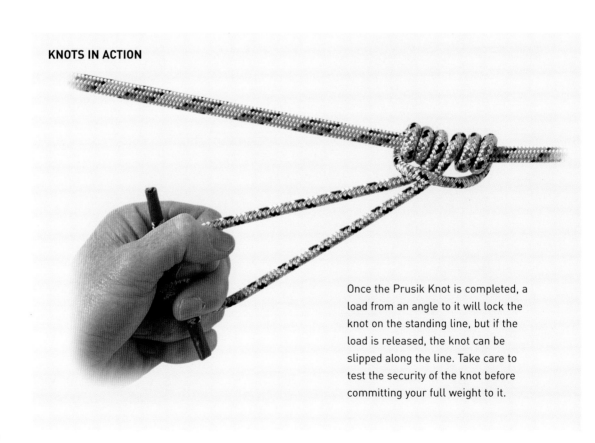

Once the Prusik Knot is completed, a load from an angle to it will lock the knot on the standing line, but if the load is released, the knot can be slipped along the line. Take care to test the security of the knot before committing your full weight to it.

2 Bring the loop up over the knotted part of the sling to enclose it.

3 Take the loop round the standing line again, laying the turn on next to, but outside the earlier turns on the line.

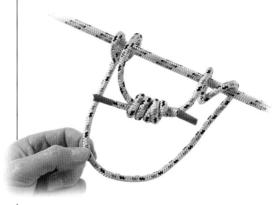

4 Take the loop back round a third time.

5 Finish by bringing the loop up over the knot.

6 Tighten by pulling on the knot. Settle the turns neatly with the knotted loop emerging from the center.

Anchor Bend

Hold-fast knots

Originally developed for securing a rope to the ring on the anchor, the Anchor Bend is a simple variation of the Round Turn and Two Half Hitches. It is an improvement in the sense that it will resist coming undone better as the load direction turns and moves about, whether it is formed on a ring or about a pole or post, making it useful in a variety of situations. It is also intended to remain in place semi-permanently, so undoing the bend can be tricky once the turns have settled down under load.

1 Start by passing the working end of the line through the ring twice from front to back to form a round turn on it.

2 Bring the working end forward and down across the standing part before tucking it up through the round turn beside the ring.

3 Again bring the working end forwards and down across the standing part, then tuck it up between itself and the standing part.

4 This process has formed a Clove Hitch about the standing part with one side locked against the ring by the round turn.

KNOTS IN ACTION

The finished Anchor Bend seen from on top with all parts worked up tight. It will hold securely as the load tightens its grip on the first part of the two half hitches (Clove Hitch), no matter from which direction the strain comes.

Klemheist Knot

The Klemheist is a variation on the Prusik Knot, also providing a way of attaching a sling to a standing rope with the ability to lock under load and slide when the load is taken off. Again the sling may be of either rope or tubular climbing tape.

1 Wrap the sling around the standing line, laying the turns side by side.

2 Put on three or four turns, working away from the direction in which the load will be applied to the sling.

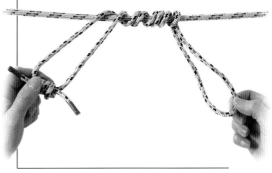

3 Pass the knotted end through the working end of the sling.

4 Bring the working end back down over the turns about the standing line.

KNOTS IN ACTION

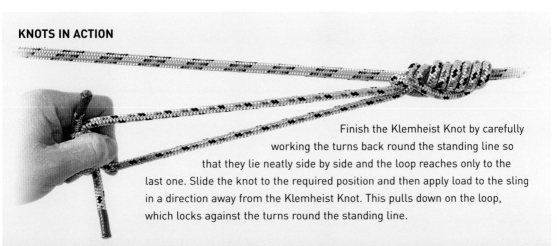

Finish the Klemheist Knot by carefully working the turns back round the standing line so that they lie neatly side by side and the loop reaches only to the last one. Slide the knot to the required position and then apply load to the sling in a direction away from the Klemheist Knot. This pulls down on the loop, which locks against the turns round the standing line.

Constrictor Knot

Developed by the great knots expert Clifford W. Ashley, the Constrictor looks much like the Clove Hitch, but it has the property of retaining any tightness worked into it. In other words, if you pull on both ends to tighten it, then let go, the knot will hold itself tight and may take a lot of work to loosen it.

1 Pass the working end of the line round the pole.

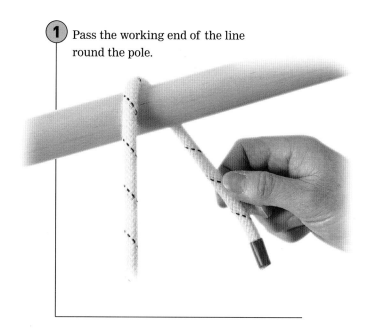

CARE AND MAINTENANCE

When a rope is cut, the end immediately starts to fray if it is not either sealed by melting or covered with a whipping. It is advisable to apply a round or two of adhesive tape to the rope, then to cut through the tape and rope and seal the end in a flame before it has a chance to fray. However, take care not to burn your fingers on a melted rope's end, it will be extremely hot and sticks to skin.

KNOTS IN ACTION

The finished, tightened, Constrictor will not loosen unintentionally and may indeed prove difficult to undo. To make this easier, you can slip the working end as in a Slipped Reef Knot. Among the Constrictor's many uses, it forms a quick and effective whipping on a rope's end.

2 Bring the end up, cross it over the first turn and send it forward under the pole.

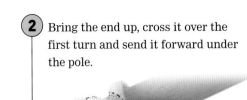

3 Cross the working end over the standing part.

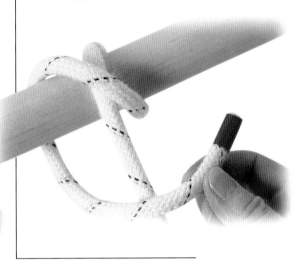

4 Tuck the working end back under the standing part where it lies beneath the crossover.

Swing Hitch

As its name suggests, this is a hitch used for setting up a children's swing. It is designed not to loosen as the loaded end of the line swings back and forth. Clearly it could be used in any situation where the load moves to and fro.

1 Lead the working end round the pole so that it points away from the standing part.

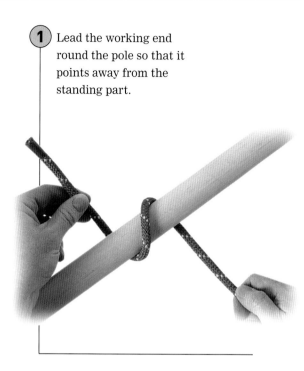

KNOTS IN ACTION

Settle the various turns to complete the Swing Hitch, making sure it retains its neat, regular form with the two "locks" holding it secure.

2 Tuck the working end forward under the part lying across the top of the pole.

3 Turn the working end back under the pole and bring it forward to tuck under itself.

4 Now dip the working end down under the standing part.

5 Bring the end up and tuck it straight through between the pole and the first crossover.

Italian Hitch

The Italian Hitch is not meant to hold a rope fixed to anything, rather it is designed to control a rope as it slides around a fixed point such as a climber's karabiner when belaying or descending. It only stays together while it is in place on a karabiner; as soon as it is removed, it falls apart.

1 Begin by forming a small crossed loop in the line, right side under left.

KNOTS IN ACTION

Once in place and settled, the Italian Hitch is ready for use. In the photograph, the load bearing part is on the right and the part on the left acts as the brake. Ease the left hand part and the load descends, its pace controlled by pulling on the brake or easing it further.

2 Form a second crossed loop; this time left side over right.

3 Turn the second loop backward so that it stands parallel to the first loop.

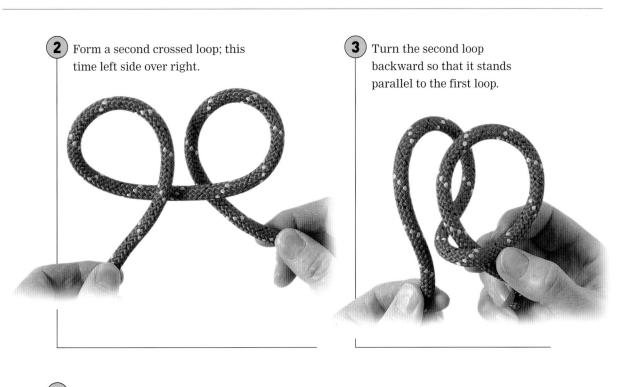

4 Slip the loops onto the karabiner with both standing parts on the same side.

5 Close the karabiner and pull the hitch tight.

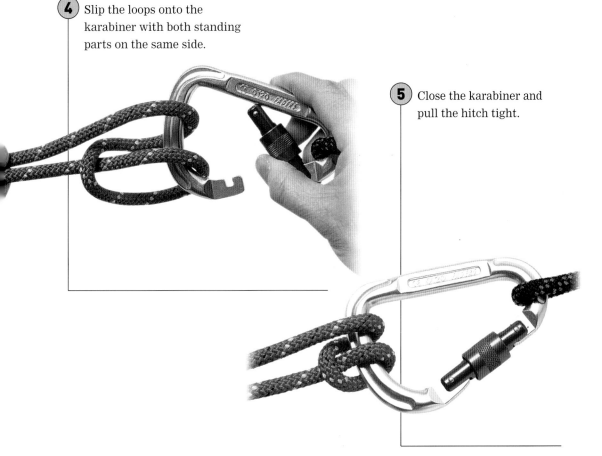

Barrel Knot

The Barrel Knot is also commonly
called the Blood Loop Dropper Knot.
The name Barrel Knot is said to
derive from the twin barrel shapes
that the knot creates. It is best
suited to use in fine monofilament
fishing lines where it offers great
security, but is almost impossible to
undo once it has been loaded. A
knife will be required to separate the
lines. For clarity, the knot is shown
here tied in cord.

1 Lie the two ends parallel to each
other, pointing in opposite
directions, and hold them tightly at
the point where you want them to be
joined.

4 Continue to spiral the working end
around the paired lines four or five
times.

KNOTS IN ACTION

Finish by threading the working end through
between its own standing part and the
standing part of the other line, making sure
that it is next to, but pointing in the opposite
direction to, the first tail end. Work the
second set of turns tight then draw the two
parts of the knot together by pulling on the
two long lines. Once all is secure and
settled, cut the tail ends off.

2 Pass the working end of the upper line down behind the lower line and loop it up across the pair of lines.

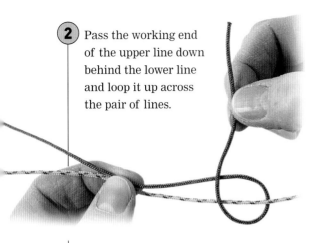

3 Send the working end back, down and around to enclose the paired lines.

5 Pass the working end back between the standing parts of the two lines.

6 Carefully work all of the turns tight and settle them down.

7 Repeat the process with the lower line, first looping it up across and down behind the upper line.

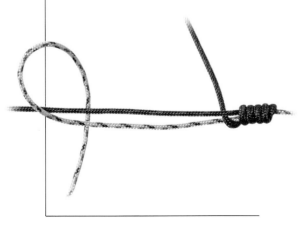

8 Wrap the working end around the paired lines four or five times, spiralling in toward the first set of turns.

Turle Knot

Apparently the Turle Knot took its name in 1884 from a Major Turle from Devon, England. It is used for tying monofilament line to hooks, though it is shown here tied in cord for clarity.

1 Thread the line through the eye of the hook before tying a Slipped Overhand Knot.

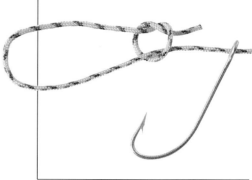

2 Pass the hook through the loop.

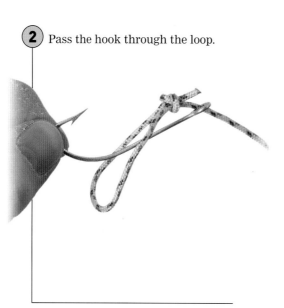

3 Tighten the knot against the shank of the hook.

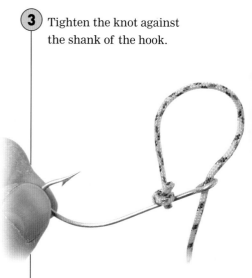

KNOTS IN ACTION

Finally pull on the line to draw the knot back along the shank to rest snugly against the eye.

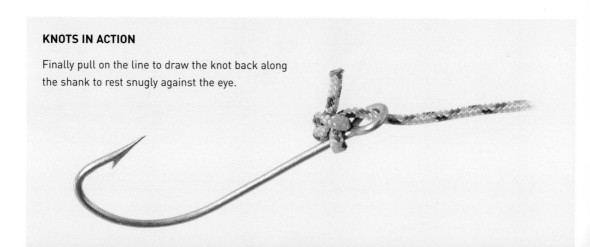

Sliding knots

Tautline Hitch

This is the ideal hitch to use on the guy ropes of a tent, fishing shelter or awning. It can be slipped up the standing part of the guy line to tension it, but then it holds in place until it's pulled back down by hand. The Tautline Hitch forms a "one way" sliding loop and is formed just as you would a Rolling Hitch (see p26) about a spar.

1 Begin by crossing the working end behind the standing part to form a loop.

CARE AND MAINTENANCE

If a rope is not in active use, it should be coiled and secured (see p16–18), so that it is ready for immediate use. When a line is left lying about it will be stepped on, which will damage it, and it will become tangled, which means it will not be ready for use. Coiling and stowing only takes seconds, but saves much time later on.

4 Lead the working end up beneath the main loop and cross it behind the standing part.

KNOTS IN ACTION

Settle all parts of the hitch down then pull the guy line tight at the peg and slide the hitch upward. While there is load on it the hitch will hold the guy taut. To slacken the guy, pull the hitch down by hand.

2 Tuck the working end down through the loop

3 Pass the working end down through the loop a second time.

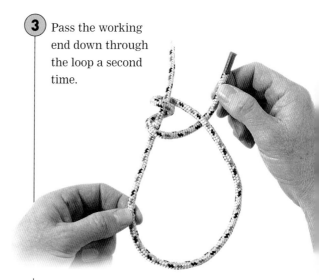

5 Bring the end forward round the standing part and tuck it downward to form a half hitch about the standing part, above the main loop.

6 Here we see the adjustable loop and the hitch ready to be settled down and tightened up.

Slip Knot

Sliding knots

This is almost identical to the Slipped Overhand Knot (p67) and is the easiest way to attach a line to a post or bar.

1 Form a crossed loop in the line so that the right part lies over the left.

KNOTS IN ACTION

The loop can be tightened by sliding the knot up towards the post or other fixed object that the loop is dropped over.

2 Pass the working end behind the loop.

3 Pull the working end up under the loop to create a smaller loop.

4 Pass the working end through the smaller loop.

5 Pull the working end to tighten the knot.

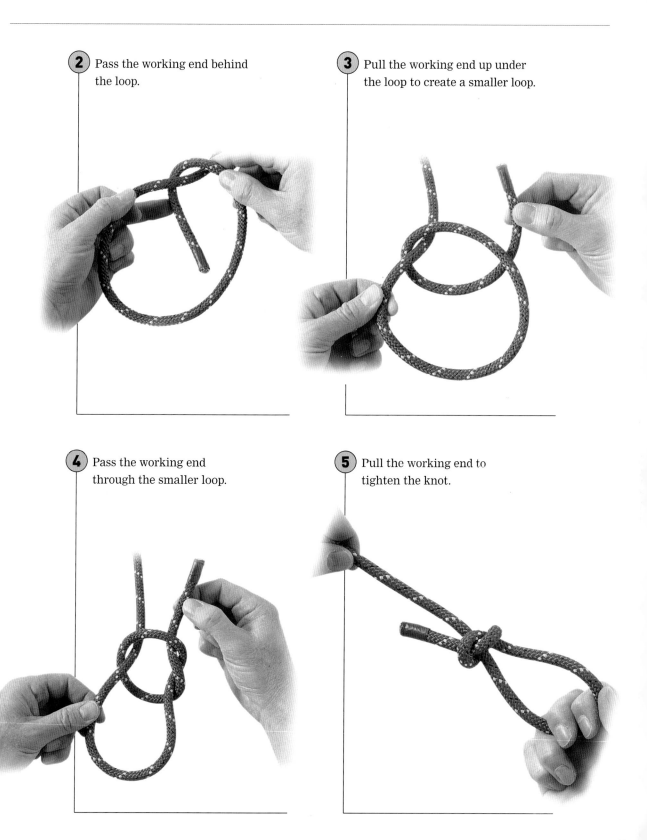

Trucker's Hitch

The Trucker's Hitch, so named because it is widely used by truck drivers to secure their loads, offers a useful 2:1 purchase (you get twice the tension for the effort you put in). It will fall apart unless there is tension on it, so untying it is no problem, but in setting the hitch up, it's important to hold all parts together carefully.

KNOTS IN ACTION

After step 3, pass the working end through a secure, fixed point, against which you can pull down. Pass the end through the loop created in step 2 and pull on the working end to tension the system. Once tensioned, you can take your hand off the hitch, as it will stay together while you heave everything down tight. To undo the hitch, just take the load off and it will fall apart. The ability to achieve a 2:1 purchase so easily, with no more equipment than a length of rope is handy in all sorts of situations where items need to be held down securely: tarpaulins, dinghies, or loose gear on a boat's deck; it's even been used to hold garden sheds down in high winds.

1 Start by securing the line to whatever is being lashed down, then, at a convenient height above the lower fixing point, form a crossed loop in the standing part of the line with the working end on top.

2 Push a bight made in the working part of the line up through the loop just formed.

3 Being careful to hold everything together, twist the lower part of the loop anti-clockwise to help hold the initial loop in place.

Slipped Overhand Knot

Many people find this an almost instinctive way to form a loop that tightens under load—a slip knot. It's clearly based on the Overhand Knot (p22) and is an easy way to attach a line to a post or bar. To undo the knot, pull the sliding part back using the short end.

KNOTS IN ACTION

The completed Slipped Overhand Knot ready for the loop to be dropped over a post or other fixed object before the knot is slid up tight.

1 Form a crossed loop in the line so that the left part lies over the right. This is done by twisting the line between your fingers.

2 Pass a bight of line from the left hand part up through the loop.

3 Push more line up through the loop to increase the size of the bight.

4 The bight now becomes a sliding loop and can be adjusted to the required size, while the overhand knot formed in the working end needs to be pulled tight to finish the knot.

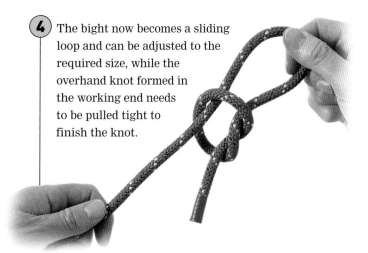

Honda Knot

The Honda Knot first provides a fixed loop, but this is quickly turned into a sliding loop, which is commonly known as a lasso or lariat. The version shown here uses an Overhand Knot as a stopper in the end of the line, as it is perhaps the quickest and easiest to tie, but some people might prefer to use a Figure-Eight Knot (see p28) instead.

1 First form an Overhand Knot in the working end of the line, then lay this end across the standing part in a crossed loop.

KNOTS IN ACTION

Once the standing part of the line has been drawn through the loop, the size of the new loop can be altered at will and, because the line is running through a fixed (small) loop, it will draw up tight instantly, for example round the neck of a steer in classic cowboy fashion.

2 Tuck the working end up through the loop and across the line on the far side to form another Overhand Knot.

3 Push the working end back up through this second Overhand Knot.

4 Pull the second Overhand Knot tight so that the first Overhand Knot in the end of the line sits snugly up against it but cannot pull out through it.

5 Pass the end of the standing part through the small loop formed at step 4 and pull the length of the line through.

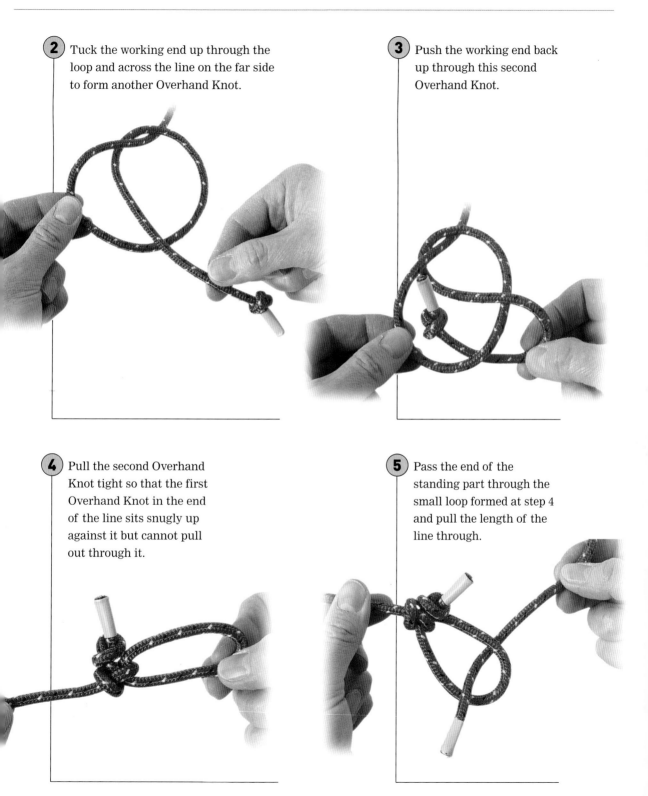

Hangman's Noose

A morbidly traditional way of forming a sliding loop, the Hangman's Noose has a gruesome history, yet remains a good-looking knot for all that. It is only included to help anyone setting up a theatrical or film scene.

1 Make two opposing loops in the rope near one end.

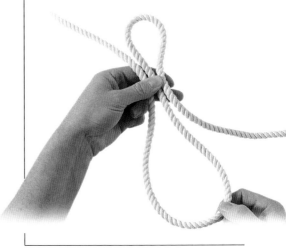

4 Continue to wrap the working end round the standing parts towards the top of one loop.

KNOTS IN ACTION

Finally pull on the fixed side of the loop and the standing part of the line to draw the small loop down onto the working end.

2 Take the working end from one loop and pass it behind the two standing parts.

3 Bring the working end up and across the front of the standing parts.

5 Some six or so turns should be laid on.

6 Finish by tucking the working end through the small loop.

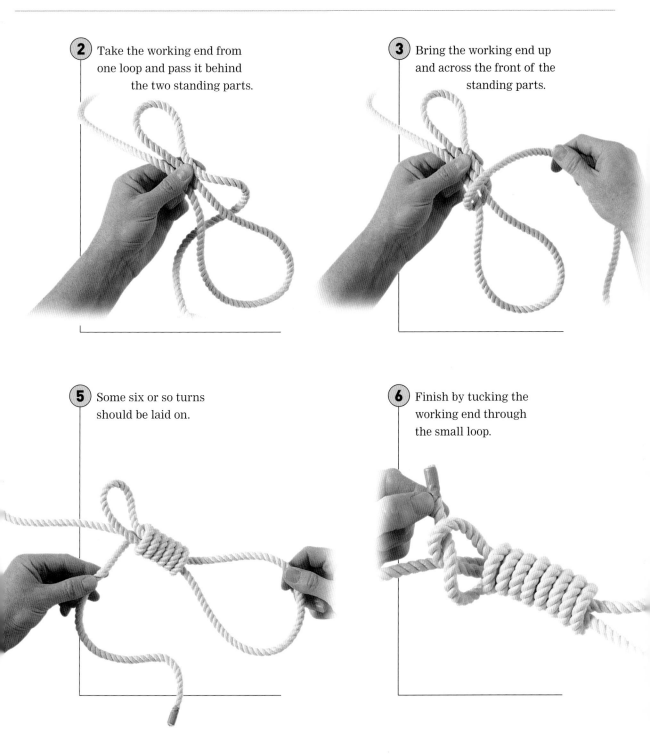

Running Bowline

The Running Bowline is rather like the Honda Knot in purpose: it provides a fixed loop through which the main part of the line can run freely, resulting in a loosely sliding loop. The Bowline itself is not usually too difficult to "break" open and undo, even when it's been drawn tight and loaded.

1 Place the working end on top of the standing part and hold the crossover between your first finger and thumb.

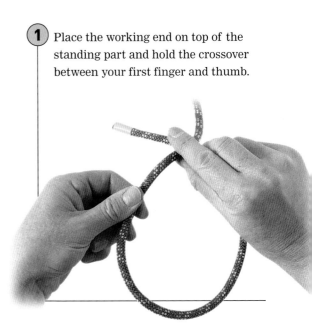

KNOTS IN ACTION

Pull the main part of the line through the small loop of the Bowline until the running loop is the size required.

2 Begin to turn your finger in toward the middle of the loop.

3 Turn your hand all the way over so that the working end of the line pokes up through a small crossed loop in the standing part of the line.

4 Pass the working end behind the standing part.

5 Bring the end forward and push it down through the loop parallel to its own standing part to complete a small Bowline.

6 Feed the standing end of the line through the small Bowline.

Sliding Figure-Eight Knots

This is a knot well suited to joining two different lines together: lines that differ in size, type or material, or even all three. It makes good use of the very basic Figure-Eight Knot and is generally quite easy to undo, even if, in extremis, you have to slide the two knots apart until they pull right off the partner rope.

1 Lay the working ends of the two lines out parallel to each other.

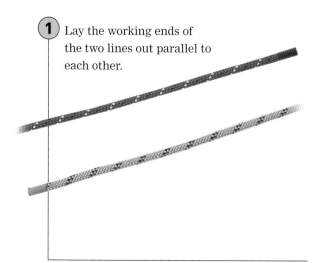

KNOTS IN ACTION

The two Figure-Eights fit neatly together but can be pulled apart even after they have been quite heavily loaded, which makes this a fairly easy way of joining and later separating two lines.

4 Settle this first Figure-Eight Knot and tighten it about the lower line.

7 Pass the working end of the lower line out through its first loop to form a Figure-Eight about the upper line and work the knot tight.

74

2 Cross the working end of the upper line down over the standing part of the lower line, then pass it up underneath the lower line and across its own standing part.

3 Still with the upper line, tuck the working end down under its own standing part and through the first loop to form a Figure-Eight Knot with the lower line passing through it.

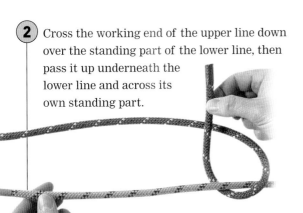

5 Working now with the lower line, pass the working end up over the standing part of the upper line, down behind it and out over its own standing part.

6 Turn the lower line's working end up behind its own standing part.

8 Each line now has a Figure of Eight Knot in its end, which encloses the other line.

9 Pull on the two standing parts and the Figure-Eights slide together.

Halter Hitch

The Halter Hitch is a refinement of the Slipped Overhand Knot that makes it easier to undo after heavy loading. It must not be confused with the Neck Halter (p87), which produces a fixed loop, suitable for use around an animal's neck. If you tried to use a Halter Hitch you would choke the poor beast when the hitch slipped tight.

1 Pass the working end of the line up through the ring, or round the pole that you want to fasten the line to, across in front of the standing part and turn it across the back of the loop now formed.

2 Push a bight of the working part down through the loop to form a Slipped Overhand Knot.

3 Tuck the tail of the line through the slip loop and work the hitch tight then slide it up against the ring.

KNOTS IN ACTION

The finished Halter Hitch all settled and worked up tight against the ring. It looks a bit of a jumble, but if the short tail is pushed back through, you have a Slipped Overhand Knot and the tail can be pulled to undo it.

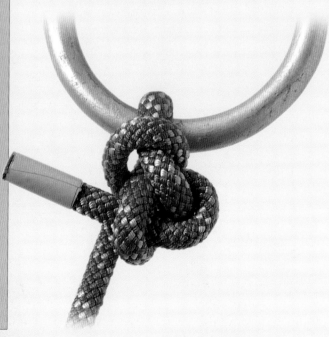

Loop knots

Bowline

The Bowline is a hugely versatile loop knot used in many different situations with many different ways of tying it. The method shown here is the one I recommend because it avoids any confusion about rabbits popping out of holes and going the wrong way round trees. Once you acquire the twist-of-the-wrist technique used in this method it is very hard to go wrong.

Just as there are many ways of tying the Bowline, there are also many ways of finishing it, but the only one worth a mention is the climbers' preference for finishing off by using the short tail to form a Half Hitch round the side of the loop next to the knot. It's a belt and braces way of making sure the Bowline won't come undone when the line is particularly slippery.

KNOTS IN ACTION

To finish the Bowline, pass the working end round behind the standing part and down through the small loop, leaving a tail of good length. The Bowline provides a quickly tied, fixed loop, especially good for tying round your own body.

1 Place the working end of the line across the standing part, forming a loop of the required size, and hold it there between first finger and thumb, finger on top.

3 Keep rolling your wrist so that the working end comes up through the big loop.

5 When you reach the point of seeing straight into the palm of your hand, the tail of the line points back along the standing part and is enclosed by a small loop of line.

2 Begin to twist your wrist so that your finger and thumb roll in toward the middle of the loop.

4 Keep twisting and a small loop forms in the standing part to enclose the working end.

The Bowline Bend just links two Bowlines together, providing an ideal way of quickly and easily joining any two ropes, no matter what their relative size or material. It's not a very good-looking union, but it works every time.

KNOTS IN ACTION

The finished Bowline Bend, which will hold no matter what the lines are made of or their relative sizes.

Bowline on the Bight

This is a sort of double Bowline in that it results in two loops of equal size. They can then be used for a variety of purposes, by providing two points to which other things can be attached or two loops to hook onto lifting points. The loops can be used to create an emergency bosun's chair for sending a person up the mast of a boat. (It's not comfortable, but it is effective in an emergency.)

KNOTS IN ACTION

The completed Bowline on the Bight with the two equal sized loops that can now form attachment points or slings.

1 Begin by doubling the line into a long bight.

4 Pull the bight well through and open it out.

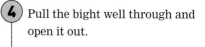

2 Apply the bight to the doubled standing part as for the Bowline.

3 Using the same twisting action as for the Bowline, turn the bight up through its own encircling loop.

5 Now pass the opened bight down over the two loops and back up to the two standing parts.

6 Bring the bight up just past the small loop it originally passed up through.

7 Pull on the two standing parts and the side of the loop linked to the bight.

8 Settle the knot firmly and separate the two loops.

Spanish Bowline

This is a very attractive, if fiddly, way of producing two fixed loops in the middle of a line. The Spanish Bowline can be useful where there is a standing line and you want to attach other lines to it, for example. It is advisable to spread loads evenly on both standing parts, so if you need two loops at the end of a line, don't use the Spanish Bowline, use a Bowline on the Bight.

1 Begin by laying out a large crossed loop at about the middle point of the line with the left hand part on top of the right. Then add two smaller crossed loops: the left loop made with the left hand part on top and the right loop with the right hand part on top. These directions are crucial, so take care.

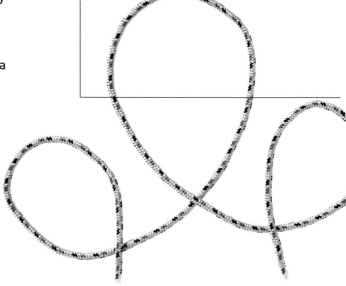

KNOTS IN ACTION

The Spanish Bowline is a good-looking knot, even if it does look a little like a startled rabbit. Note its symmetry, which is always a good check that it is correctly formed. Be sure to adjust the length of the "ears" before settling the knot firmly as it is not the easiest to loosen once loaded.

2 Now fold the large loop down over the two smaller ones.

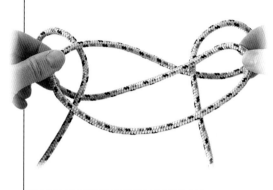

3 Spread the folded-down, large loop so that it encloses the two smaller loops.

4 Lift the two smaller loops out to lie on top of the big loop so that you can pull the "corners" of the big loop up through the small ones.

5 Pull the big loop out into two "ears" and adjust them to the required sizes, if necessary, by working line through the whole knot.

6 Settle the knot by pulling on both ears together and on the two standing parts of the line.

7 The completed Spanish Bowline ready for use.

Man Harness

The Man Harness is used to put a loop in a line at any chosen distance from the ends and it can be formed while the ends of the rope are fixed. A series of these loops can be used to create a rudimentary ladder, but use good, strong rope, as the tight turns within the knot will reduce its ultimate strength substantially.

1 Form a clockwise crossed loop with the working part passing over the standing part and then crossing behind the loop.

2 Push the lower side of the loop upward behind the former working part.

3 Pull this bight up in front of the upper section of the original loop.

4 Keep pulling upward to tighten the knot and form a larger loop, adjusting its size as necessary by feeding line through the knot.

KNOTS IN ACTION

The completed Man Harness is pulled up tight once the size of the loop has been adjusted to suit requirements. It can be used as a harness or as an attachment point.

Englishman's Loop

Where the Fisherman's Knot (p96) is tied with two sliding Overhand Knots, the Englishman's Loop is tied with an Overhand Knot and a Slipped Overhand Knot drawn together to give a fixed loop. It's very simple to tie and pulls apart to untie quite easily.

1 Form a crossed loop in the line, right side under left.

2 Push a bight of the right-hand part through the loop to make a Slipped Overhand Knot.

3 Pull the knot tight then pass the tail of the slipped loop round behind the standing part.

4 Bring the end forward and tuck it down through the loop just formed in itself to make an Overhand Knot about the standing part.

KNOTS IN ACTION

Tighten the knot around the standing part, and then pull on the loop to slide the Overhand Knot up against its companion, finishing the whole Englishman's Loop.

Figure-Eight Loop

This provides an excellent way of placing a loop at some distance along the length of a rope, rather than right at one end. It is easy to tie, is generally not too hard to untie once it's been loaded, and is used a lot by climbers.

KNOTS IN ACTION

The Figure-Eight Loop is suitable for use in all sizes of line and generally remains easy to untie after it's been used.

1 Form a bight in the line at whatever point you want the loop to be.

2 Twist the bight round and lay it across the standing parts of the line.

3 Pass the bight back and up behind the standing parts.

4 Turn the bight across in front of itself and push it down through the first loop.

5 Finally, pull the bight through to form the size of loop required and settle the various parts down. Pull tight.

Neck Halter

The Neck Halter can either be tied and then dropped over the animal's head, or it can be tied to fit around the neck. The method shown here pre-ties the loop. To tie the halter around an animal's neck, first form the Figure-Eight Knot then pass the end of the rope round the animal's neck, down through the Figure-Eight and finish with an Overhand Knot.

KNOTS IN ACTION

To complete the Neck Halter, pull on the loop so that the Overhand Knot settles against the Figure-Eight Knot. The Neck Halter is suitable for use on horses, cows and other animals. It provides a fixed loop, which is adjustable once it has been formed, by moving the Overhand Knot.

1 To pre-tie the halter, start by putting an Overhand Knot in the end of the rope.

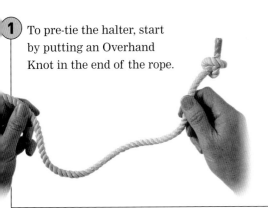

2 Form a loop in the line, then take the working end back across the standing part.

3 Form a second loop to create the Figure-Eight.

4 Push a loop of the rope through the first part of the Eight shape.

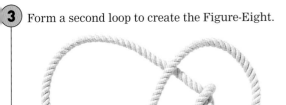

5 Work the Figure-Eight tight around the sliding part of the loop.

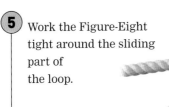

Blood Loop Dropper Knot

Clearly based on the Blood Knot, this knot produces a fixed loop on one side of a line, which is used by fly fishermen for tying on extra flies called "droppers." While its name seems to have standardized in this form, its origin and intended purpose would be clearer if it were known as the Dropper Loop Blood Knot. Although shown here tied in cord for clarity, it is another knot ideally suited to use with fine monofilament line.

1 Start by forming quite a large, loose Overhand Knot.

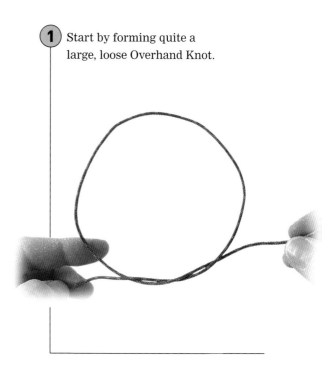

KNOTS IN ACTION

Work the twists up into tight turns against the neck of the loop and pull the line out straight to help tighten everything. Unpicking this knot is very hard once it has been put under load.

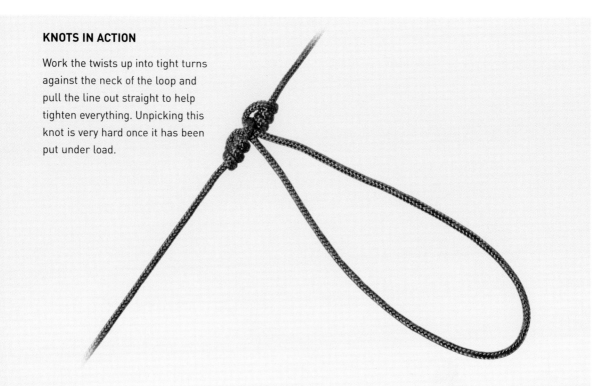

2 Now continue twisting the working
end around the loop several times.

3 Count in from each end to
find the middle turn and
open it up.

4 Pass a bight of the upper,
single loop strand down
through the opened twist.

5 Pull the bight through to
form a loop and slide the
twists together.

6 With the bight drawn
well through to form a
large loop, settle the
twists into place.

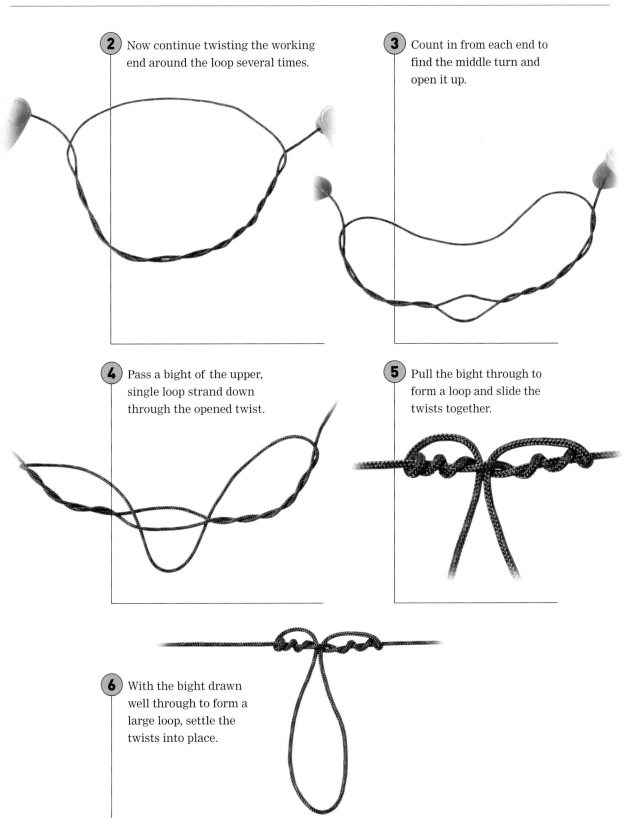

Angler's Loop

The Angler's Loop is a nice-looking, symmetrical knot, producing a fixed loop. It is suitable for use in all types of rope and will also work well with monofilament line, which makes it suitable for many fishing purposes. Like so many other knots there are several ways to tie it, as it starts with a Slipped Overhand Knot, but the "threaded" way shown here keeps the whole process clear.

KNOTS IN ACTION

To finish the Angler's Loop, work all parts tight after adjusting the loop to the required size. Once settled, the knot will not slip, but remains fairly easy to undo.

1 Pass the working end of the line under the standing part, cross up over it and tuck it down through the loop to make an Overhand Knot.

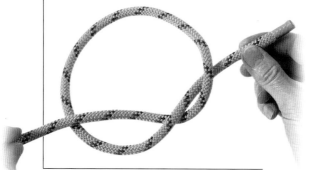

2 Send the working end back up through the loop beside itself to form a Slipped Overhand Knot.

3 Take the working end down behind the standing part and up between the parts forming the crossover of the Overhand Knot.

4 Lead the working end across over the standing part and out between the sides of the two loops.

Knots **for joining ropes**

Sheet Bend

The Sheet Bend is a perfect example of how knots, bends, and hitches use friction and bind one part of the rope against another to achieve and maintain a secure lock. All that happens in this simple bend is that the load binds one part against another where they cross. To undo the bend all you have to do is release the tension. The Sheet Bend is used to join two ropes together, whether they are of equal or different size.

KNOTS IN ACTION

Finish the Sheet Bend by settling the turns down and applying tension. Once settled, the bend will usually stay together, but tension is required to be sure of security.

1 Form a loop in the end of one rope, the larger if they are not the same size, and pass the end of the other rope up through it.

2 Lead the end across the top of the loop and down behind both parts of it.

3 Bring the end to the front and pass it up between its own standing part and the loop.

Double Sheet Bend

If the lines being joined together are particularly springy, then instead of using the single Sheet Bend, it is wise to add an extra turn to make it into a Double Sheet Bend. This little bit of extra security is something of an insurance policy—you hope it won't be needed, but it's there if you do.

1 Form a loop in the larger rope, if the two are different sizes. Pass the working end of the second line up through the loop, down behind the paired standing parts, up across the loop, beneath its own standing part, to form a single Sheet Bend.

2 Pass the working end down behind the loop and then bring it up across the front, again passing beneath its own standing part, so that there is a double turn about the loop.

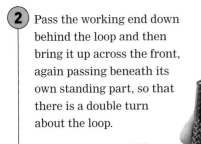

KNOTS IN ACTION

To finish the Double Sheet Bend, settle all the parts down closely and apply load to the two lines. It is almost as easy to form as the basic Sheet Bend, but there is an element of extra security.

Carrick Bend

The Carrick Bend is a very good, secure way of joining two ropes together. It works whether the lines are of the same size or not. Unusually, this bend can, instead of being used as a joining knot, be left at the flat stage and turned into a mat by doubling or tripling the turns it is made up from.

1 Form a crossed loop in the end of the larger rope by laying the end across on top of the standing part.

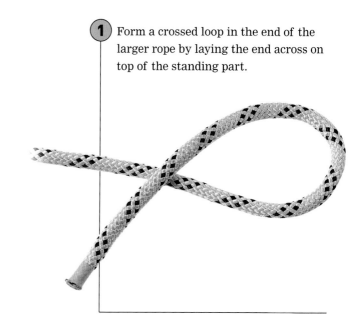

KNOTS IN ACTION

To finish the Carrick Bend, keep drawing all parts together until the body of the bend moves from being flat to being a cube. The main lengths of the two ropes should emerge opposite each other and the two tails should come out at right angles to each other and also to their own standing parts.

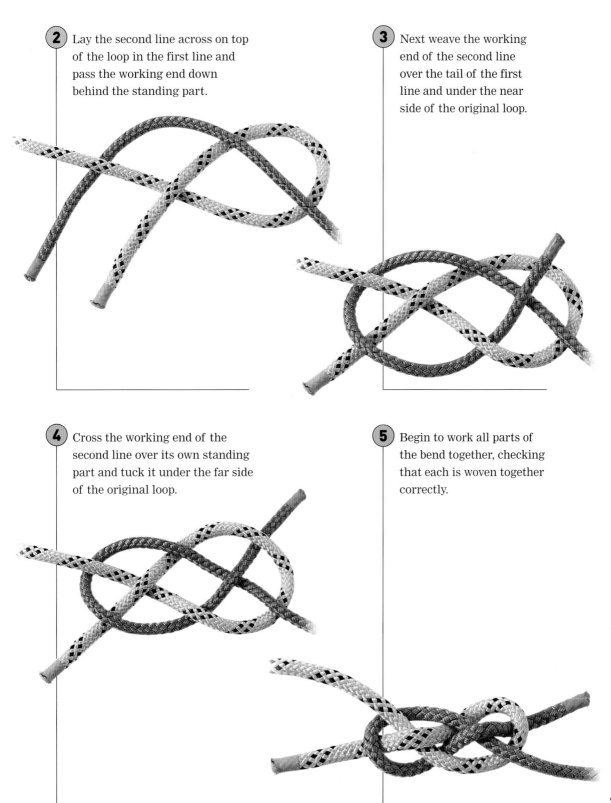

2 Lay the second line across on top of the loop in the first line and pass the working end down behind the standing part.

3 Next weave the working end of the second line over the tail of the first line and under the near side of the original loop.

4 Cross the working end of the second line over its own standing part and tuck it under the far side of the original loop.

5 Begin to work all parts of the bend together, checking that each is woven together correctly.

Fisherman's Knot

The Fisherman's Knot consists of a pair of sliding Overhand Knots, each formed about the other line. Though it can be used in most sizes and types of line, this knot is ideally suited to monofilament fishing line (hence its name), but once tightened and loaded, in that material, it may well prove impossible to undo. A sharp knife may be the only answer for separating the lines.

1 Lay the ends of the two lines down parallel to each other, pointing in opposite directions.

4 Now, using the lower (second) line, pass the working end up behind the standing part of the upper line then down across it and across its own standing part.

KNOTS IN ACTION

Pull on the two standing parts to slide the two Overhand Knots together and settle them against each other. Loading the lines will draw them close together and they may prove hard to untie when finished with.

2 Starting with the upper line, turn the working end down across the lower line and bring it up behind that line and its own standing part.

3 Bring the working end down across its own standing part and tuck it down through the loop to form the first Overhand Knot.

5 Tuck the working end up through the loop to complete the second Overhand Knot.

6 Each line now has an Overhand Knot in its working end and its standing part is enclosed by an Overhand Knot. To complete the Fisherman's Knot, pull on the two standing parts.

Double Fisherman's Knot

This is an excellent knot for joining two lines, whether you are an angler or a climber, for although it is quite a bulky knot, it holds well in a wide variety of materials. It should be used if the slippery nature of the lines gives rise to any doubts about the security of a simple Fisherman's Knot.

1 Lay the ends of the two lines down parallel to each other, pointing in opposite directions, then turn the working end of the lower line up over the upper line, down behind both lines and up across the front of both before crossing down between the front and back parts.

4 Begin the second part of the knot by passing the working end of the upper line down in front of the standing part of the lower line, back up behind both lines, down across the front of both and out, backward, between the lower side of the loop just formed and the standing part of the lower line.

KNOTS IN ACTION

To complete the Double Fisherman's Knot, pull on the two standing parts to draw the two knots tightly together. If you want to stop the two tail ends catching on anything, just tape them to their neighboring standing parts.

2 Now weave the working end up over the lower side of the left hand loop and out through it, parallel to the standing part of the upper line.

3 Pull on both the working end and the standing part to settle knot together.

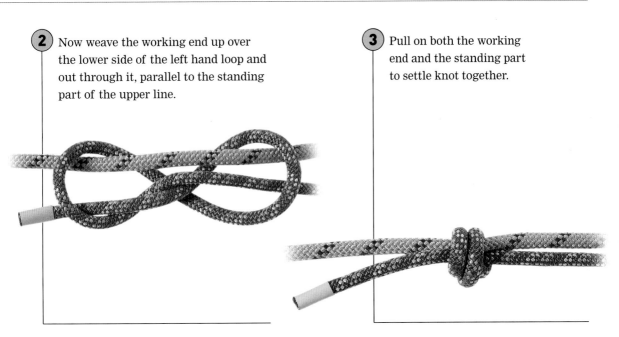

5 Bring the working end forward again and send it out between the upper part of the loop and the standing part of the lower line, parallel to that standing part.

6 Pull on both the standing part and the working end to settle the knot and tighten it.

Double Grinner Knot

The Double Grinner Knot is used for joining two fine monofilament lines, usually for fly-fishing, and consists of a pair of Grinner Knots tied about the pair of lines. The illustrations show the knot tied in cord only for clarity.

1 First pair the lines with the ends lying in opposite directions, then turn the upper line back in a loop and tuck the working end round the pair of lines and out through the loop.

VARIATION: The Grinner Knot is used for tying monofilament line to a fishing hook, but is shown here, tied in cord, for clarity. It is a straightforward and popular knot, but another that is unlikely to untie after use; it will probably have to be cut through.

a) Thread the line through the eye of the hook and lead it back parallel to the standing part, then bring it toward the hook again in a loop. Turn the working end down across both parts and back up behind them.

b) Pass the working end forward through the loop, down across the pair of standing parts and make a series of turns around the paired lines, within the big loop. About four turns should be sufficient.

c) To finish the Grinner Knot, work all the turns up tight and settle the loop over them by pulling on the standing part of the line, which also snugs the knot up against the eye of the hook.

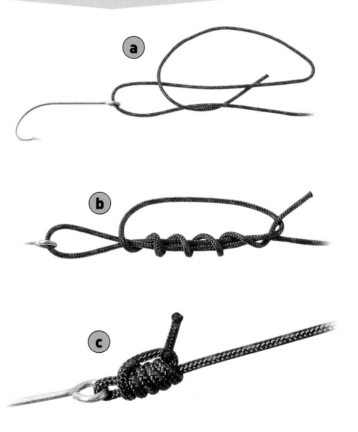

2 Continue to bind the paired lines together, using the working end of the upper line.

3 Tighten the first knot, settling the turns side by side.

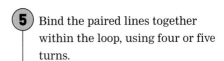

4 Repeat the process with the lower line, first forming a loop with the working end back towards the first knot. Turn the working end across the paired lines and tuck it round the back and out through the front of the loop.

5 Bind the paired lines together within the loop, using four or five turns.

6 Settle the second knot down, tightening it evenly.

KNOTS IN ACTION

The two knots are drawn together by pulling on the two standing parts. This completes the Double Grinner Knot and joins the two lines strongly and durably.

Hunter's Bend

The Hunter's Bend is particularly good for tying together two lines made from rather slippery materials. It gained its current name in 1978 when it was attributed to Dr Edward Hunter. Prior to that it had been an obscure bend known as the Rigger's Bend.

1 Bring the working ends of the two lines together, but pointing in opposite directions.

2 Form a crossed loop using the paired lines with the left hand pair on top.

3 Bring the right hand working end up over the paired parts and tuck it backward through the loop.

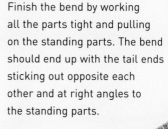

4 Now tuck the other working end up from behind the loop. The two working ends should now be tucked through from opposite sides of the loop and be pointing out in opposite directions.

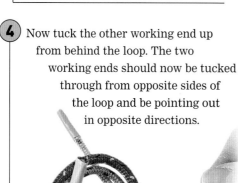

KNOTS IN ACTION

Finish the bend by working all the parts tight and pulling on the standing parts. The bend should end up with the tail ends sticking out opposite each other and at right angles to the standing parts.

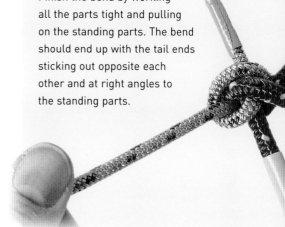

Figure-Eight Bend

This bend provides yet another use for the basic Figure-Eight. In this instance a Figure-Eight is formed in the end of one line and the end of the other line is threaded back along a reciprocal path through it. The finished knot is just a double-stranded Figure-Eight linking the two ropes.

KNOTS IN ACTION

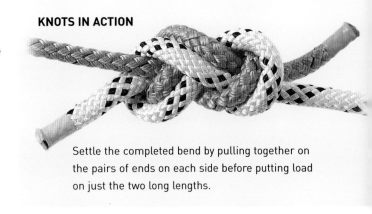

Settle the completed bend by pulling together on the pairs of ends on each side before putting load on just the two long lengths.

1 Form the initial Figure-Eight by turning the end of one line back across the standing part to form a crossed loop and then pass the end up underneath the standing part.

2 Bring the working end down across the near side of the loop then pass it down and out under the far side of the loop to form the Figure-Eight.

3 Leaving that first Figure-Eight loose, thread the working end of the second line in parallel to the tail of the first line and begin to follow it round behind the standing part of the first line.

4 Tuck the working end of the second rope up across the loop, passing it underneath the doubled crossing strands.

5 Finally thread the working end of the second line back through, parallel to the standing part of the first line to completely double the Figure-Eight.

Water Knot

The Water Knot is also known as the Tape Knot, because it is ideal for linking the tapes favored by climbers. It is also known as the Doubled Overhand Knot, because it is an Overhand Knot doubled by threading the second line back along the path of the first. It is a very secure knot, even in lines of differing sizes, but for added security an extra turn can be added, as is done for the Surgeon's Knot.

KNOTS IN ACTION

The finished Water Knot is worked tight by pulling all four ends together, then by loading the two lines. If it is used for joining climbing tapes, be sure to thread the second tape round so that it remains on the same side of the first throughout, as shown with the rope in photo 4.

1 Form a loop with the working end and tuck it through to make an Overhand Knot.

2 Take the working end of the second line and thread it back into the knot beginning at the tail end of the first line.

3 Follow all the way round the first knot, forming a second, parallel knot.

4 Bring the working end out along the standing part of the first line to complete a second Overhand Knot paralleling the first.

Shortening knots

Chain Knot

Chain plaiting (properly known as a chain sennit) is often used in decorative ropework, for example in lanyards, but is also a way of shortening a rope. It will do nothing for the overall strength of the line, but because of the way each part is linked, it remains easy to undo after the first knot has been freed.

1 Begin by forming a crossed loop, right side under left.

4 Pass the new bight through the slipped bight already formed.

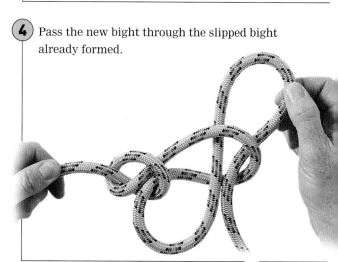

KNOTS IN ACTION

Be sure to pass the bights through in the same direction each time. Continue until the chain is the required length (or the line has been shortened sufficiently) and then finish off by passing the end of the line (rather than another bight) through the last loop and pull everything tight. To undo the chain, unpick that last link and then a good pull on the right hand part will unravel the whole chain.

2 Push a bight of the right hand part down through the loop to form a Slipped Overhand Knot.

3 Form another bight in the right hand part.

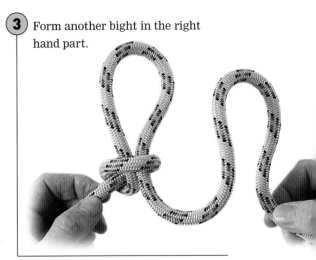

5 Pull the bight to tighten the knot and already the shape of the chain begins to be seen.

6 Continue passing bights formed in the right hand part back through the previous bight. Then, to finish, pass the end of the line back through the last loop.

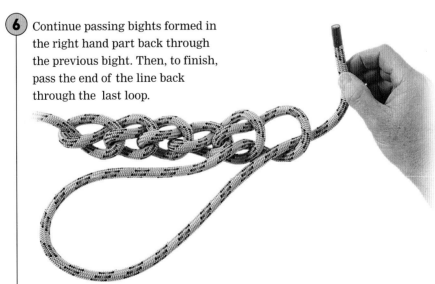

Sheepshank

The Sheepshank is the usual way of shortening a rope without cutting it. Provided there is a load on each end, the Sheepshank will remain securely in place, but as soon as the tension is released, it will fall apart. If it is to be left in place for any length of time and the strain may come and go it is wise to tie the "ears" to the single lines.

1 Lay the line out in two opposing parallel bights.

2 Form a crossed loop in the upper part, left end on top.

3 Push the lower bight back through the loop. This direction is crucial.

4 Form a crossed loop in the lower part of the line, right hand end on top.

5 Push the upper bight back through this loop. Again, the direction is crucial.

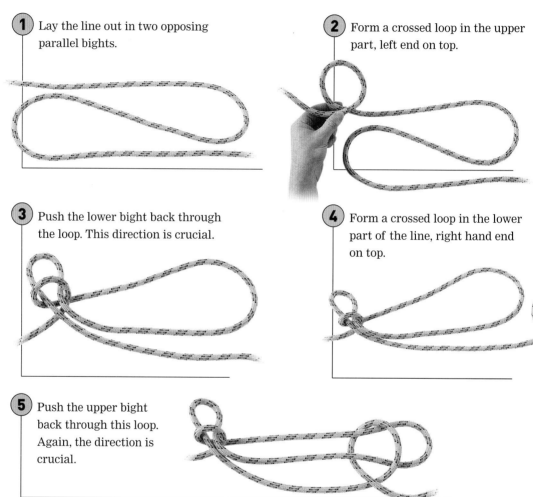

KNOTS IN ACTION

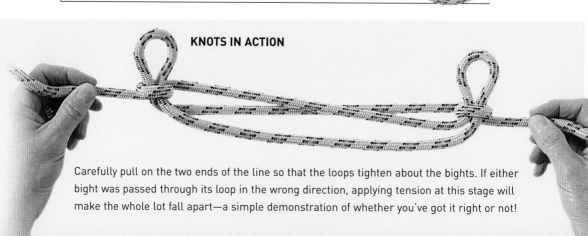

Carefully pull on the two ends of the line so that the loops tighten about the bights. If either bight was passed through its loop in the wrong direction, applying tension at this stage will make the whole lot fall apart—a simple demonstration of whether you've got it right or not!

Weight-adding knots

Stevedore Knot

Like the Heaving Line Knot, the Stevedore Knot is used to put weight in the end of a heaving line or as a Stopper Knot. It is very similar to the Heaving Line Knot, but the spiralling turns run back down the line not up over the loop, making it more akin to a Figure-Eight.

1 Start by crossing the working end over the standing part to form a crossed loop.

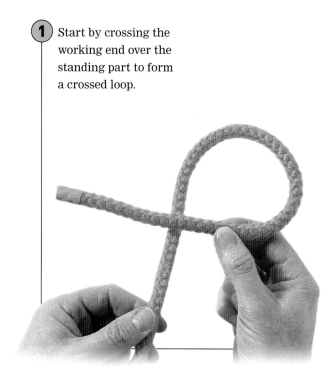

KNOTS IN ACTION

To finish the Stevedore Knot, settle the turns together and then pull on the standing part to close the loop about the tail end and tighten the whole knot together.

2 Now pass the working end across behind the standing part.

3 Take the working end across the front of the standing part again.

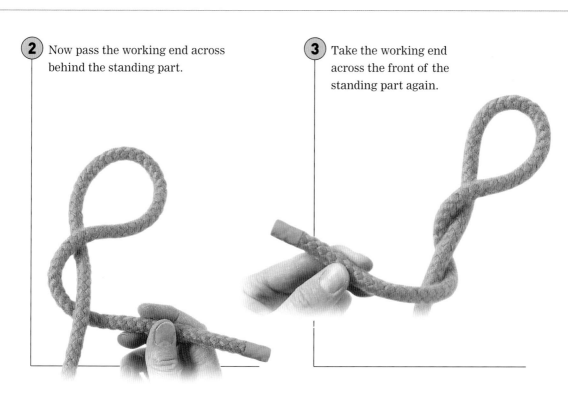

4 Cross the working end behind the standing part a second time and lead it up to the loop.

5 Pass the working end back through the loop to complete the knot.

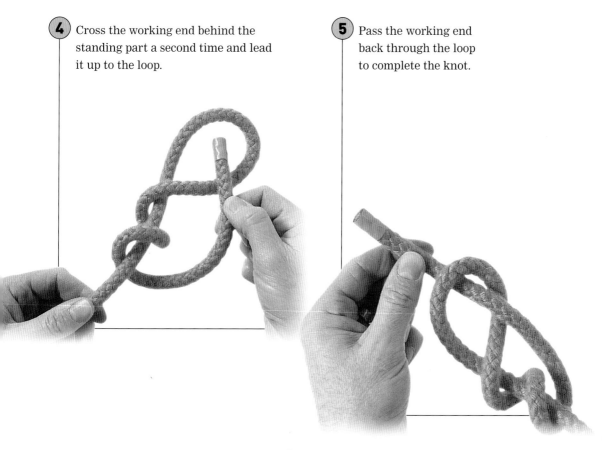

Monkey's Fist

This is the sailor's traditional way of creating a heavy, but decorative, knot in the end of a heaving line. For added weight it is common to insert a wooden ball or stone into the center of the fist before tightening it all up. As a purely decorative knot the Monkey's Fist is found in all sorts of places including lanyards, key fobs and bell ropes. Only trial and error will show how much line is needed to form the fist and hence how far from the end of the line to start.

1 Form a loop in the line, toward the end where you want the Monkey's Fist to be, but using a long length of line (enough to complete the knot). Depending upon the type of line used, it may be necessary to form the loops around your fingers. This fairly stiff line allowed the loops to stand on their own.

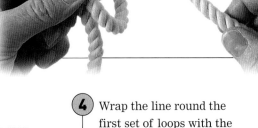

4 Wrap the line round the first set of loops with the same number of turns.

KNOTS IN ACTION

The finished Monkey's Fist is left permanently in the line, as it is too fiddly to tie each time it's needed.

2 Depending upon the size of line in use, make two or three complete turns, working toward the end of the line.

3 Holding the completed loops tightly, turn the line at right angles and begin to wrap it around the first set of loops, being careful to retain their shape.

5 Push the working end back through the first set of loops above the wrapping turns.

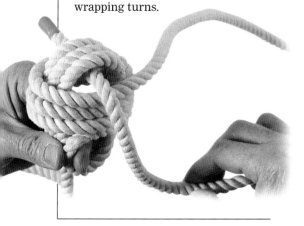

6 Bring the working end forward through the lower part of the first set of loops, below the wrapping turns.

7 Tuck the working end through again above the wrapping turns and continue for the same number of turns as in each previous stage.

8 If you want to insert a weight, do so now before carefully working the fist tight. The tail end may either be cut short, whipped and tucked into the fist or it can be spliced or seized to the main part of the line.

Stopper Knot

When a rope needs to be prevented from passing through a large eye or could do with a bit of weight in the end, perhaps to help when it's thrown, this Stopper Knot is a good bet. The way it's formed looks a bit tricky as it has to be wrapped round your fingers, but actually it's quite easy and, of course, gets easier with practice.

KNOTS IN ACTION

The Stopper Knot is a handsome, symmetrical knot that adds a fair bit of weight to the rope's end, although weight than can be increased by putting on extra turns.

1 Use your first two fingers to wrap turns of the line round; they seem to be the right size for almost all lines.

4 Put a second turn on parallel to the first.

7 Bring the working end forward beneath your fingers then slip the loops off them and push the working end through the hole left in the middle.

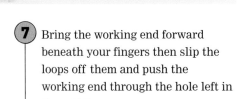

8 The working end is passed right through the center to emerge at the end opposite the standing part.

2 Take the working end of the line over the top of your fingers, down behind them and forward underneath to cross up over their front.

3 Cross the working part over the standing part and turn it around your fingers.

5 Then put on a third turn next to the second.

6 A fourth turn is usually enough to give a fairly bulky knot.

9 Gently remove the slack from the turns, working them tight so that they lie neatly parallel to each other.

10 With the turns worked tight and the crossover between standing part and working end pulled tight in the middle of the knot it is completed.

Heaving Line Knot

As its name suggests, this is a knot designed to be tied in the end of a heaving line, which is a light messenger line thrown from one point to another and then used to pull a heavier line across. It's quite bulky and adds a reasonable amount of weight, which helps the line to 'fly' further. It will never be under load, so it should remain easy to undo.

KNOTS IN ACTION

The finished knot should have a neat, spiralled appearance. In addition to being used in the end of a heaving line, this knot works well as a bulky stopper knot to prevent a line running through an eye or block.

1 Begin by forming a crossed loop with the working end crossing down behind the standing part.

2 Bring the working end forward and up to cross over the loop.

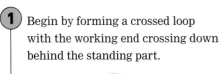

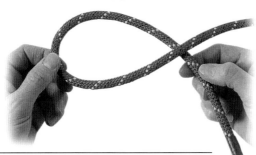

3 Pass the working end down behind the loop and up across the front again.

4 Continue putting similar clockwise turns on until about four have been completed, then tuck the working end through the loop.

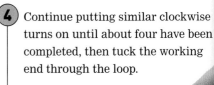

5 Pull the working end through and settle the turns then draw the loop tight by pulling on the standing part.

Lashings

Cross Lashing

This is a way of binding two poles together at right angles so that they will not slip and twist. It remains easy to undo, as there is nothing to bind.

1 Begin by laying the poles across each other at right angles and tie a Constrictor Knot (p50) about the lower one.

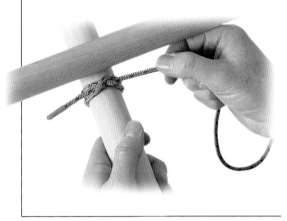

KNOTS IN ACTION

Slide the Clove Hitch up against the binding turns and work it tight. Provided that the lashing is put on tightly, there will be very little load on the Clove Hitch and it will not work loose. If the lashing needs to be tightened further, lay on several turns around it at 90 degrees, passing between the poles. These turns will push the poles apart, effectively tightening the lashings themselves and are very effective.

2 Pass the long working end of the binding rope back over the upper pole, down behind the lower one, then up and over the upper one.

3 Take the working end down under the lower pole and begin again, going back over the upper pole, down under the lower pole and forward over the upper pole.

4 With the pattern of turns established, follow round again, making sure each turn is laid close beside the previous one and that it is pulled as tight as possible.

5 With several turns completed, take a turn on the upper pole with the working end coming up on the inside of the turn.

6 Cross the working end outward, pass it down round the pole and back up under itself to form a Clove Hitch about the upper pole.

Parallel Lashing

This is a way of binding a pair of poles securely together, either to strengthen one that is damaged or to double them up or to form a pair of sheerlegs (an A-frame).

1 Lay the poles parallel to one another and tie a Constrictor Knot (p60) about the lower one at the point where the lashing is to begin.

4 When sufficient turns are in place, pass the working end down between the poles.

5 Now turn at right angles and lead the working part across the turns that bind the poles together.

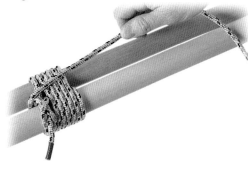

KNOTS IN ACTION

Once the poles have been lashed together, they can be twisted to form an A-frame or pair of sheerlegs, which is why this lashing is sometimes known as a sheer lashing.

8 Pass the working end around one pole and tuck it under itself.

2 Use the long working end of the line to start putting on the binding turns to lash the two poles together.

3 Several turns will be needed to hold the poles together, the number being judged according to the purpose of the lashing.

6 Pass the working end down between the poles again.

7 Bring the working end up and put on three or four turns around the lashing, between the poles. Tuck the right end down behind the left end and bring it forward through the center of the knot.

9 Pass the end round the pole again and tuck it under itself to complete a Clove Hitch around the pole.

10 Work the Clove hitch tight to keep it secure. The turns put on around the lashing turns serve to tighten the whole lashing considerably and relieve load on the Clove Hitch.

Transom Knot

This is a great way of tying small diameter poles together. For example, it's a quick and straightforward way of setting up fruit canes, bean poles or trellis battens.

1 Cross the poles, one on top of the other and run the rope along the lower pole, over the crossed one, down and around the lower pole. Lead it across over its own standing part, down and behind the lower pole.

2 Pass the working end between the crossed parts.

KNOTS IN ACTION

With the knot tightened and settled, the ends can be trimmed off. The Transom Knot does not have the ultimate security or rigidity of a Square Lashing, but it is quick and good enough for light duties.

3 Tuck the working end back beneath the standing part.

4 Pull the end through to tighten. Work the line round all parts, to tighten it and pull on both ends to settle it all down, making sure that the overhand part lies beneath the crossover.

Decorative knots

Turk's Head

The Turk's Head is a purely decorative knot used in all sorts of fancywork from tiller decoration to bell ropes and bangles. It can be tied with many different numbers of twists and turns and can have any number of parallel lines running through it. The version shown here is one of the simplest, showing the general form very clearly. The Turk's Head can be formed about one of the tier's hands so that it ends up as a stand-alone knot (when it can, for example, be opened out as a mat) or, as here, it can be tied about an object. In this case the knot can be slipped off the pole when finished or left in place as part of a decoration.

1 Pass the working end back over the pole, forward underneath, across the standing part and back down behind the pole.

4 Lift the right hand part over the left.

KNOTS IN ACTION

That completes the first stage of the Turk's Head. Now continue using the working end to follow round the whole knot, paralleling the line it is now lying next to. Be sure to parallel the line; don't cross it. Once the knot has been doubled, the ends are cut short and seized together inside the knot.

2 Bring the working end up in front of the pole and tuck it underneath the crossing part to complete a Clove Hitch about the pole.

3 Roll the Clove Hitch round the pole so that the back faces you with the working end pointing down.

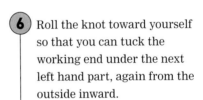

5 Bring the working end up and tuck it under the new right hand part from the outside inward.

6 Roll the knot toward yourself so that you can tuck the working end under the next left hand part, again from the outside inward.

7 Turn the knot toward yourself again and tuck the working end under the next right hand part, also from the outside inward so that it is now running parallel, but in opposition to the standing part.

True Lover's Knot

The True Lover's Knot is used in decorative ropework as a symbol of true and undying love, each of the interlinked Overhand Knots mirroring its companion. The knot is useful in linking parallel lines for decorated items such as lanyards. The True Lover's Knot is not to be used for joining ropes where there is any question of strength being involved; it is a linking rather than joining knot.

KNOTS IN ACTION

Finish the True Lover's Knot by working everything up tight so that the knots lie snugly together in harmonious union!

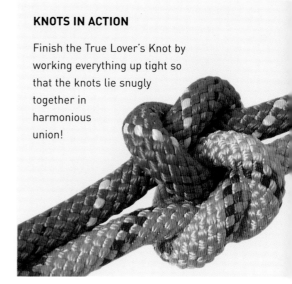

1 Form an Overhand Knot in the first line at the required position along its length, then feed the working end of the second line up through the loop, paralleling the first line.

2 Bring the working end of the second line across the top of its own standing part.

3 Tuck the working end up through the loop to form the second Overhand Knot.

4 Begin to tighten the knot by pulling on all four ends together.

Index